Wakefield Press

For the Love of Rhinos
(and this life)

Born and educated in Adelaide, Heather Caddick has had a diverse career spanning kindergarten teaching to stockbroking and investment. She has always been passionate about voluntary work, encompassing conservation of wildlife and humanitarian causes in Africa.

When she is not travelling, she lives in Adelaide with her husband, Alfie.

For the Love of Rhinos

(and this life)

Heather Caddick

Wakefield Press

Wakefield Press
16 Rose Street
Mile End
South Australia 5031
www.wakefieldpress.com.au

First published 2015

Copyright © Heather Caddick, 2015

All rights reserved. This book is copyright. Apart from any fair dealing for the purposes of private study, research, criticism or review, as permitted under the Copyright Act, no part may be reproduced without written permission. Enquiries should be addressed to the publisher.

Edited by Julia Beaven, Wakefield Press
Designed by Liz Nicholson, designBITE
Printed in Australia by Ligare Pty Ltd

National Library of Australia Cataloguing-in-Publication entry

Creator:	Caddick, Heather, 1944– , author.
Title:	For the love of rhinos (and this life) / Heather Caddick.
ISBN:	978 1 74305 353 9 (hardback).
Subjects:	Caddick, Heather, 1944– .
	Caddick, Heather, 1944– – Travel.
	Human ecology.
	Wildlife conservation.
	Short stories.
Dewey Number:	304.2

Contents

Preface   vii

Outback Cattle Drive, Riding with Drovers   1

For the Love of Rhinos   6

The Relevance of Zoos Today   11

Annapurna Trek   14

Soweto by Tuk Tuk   18

Middle East Hijinks and Hijacks   21

Swedish Smorgasbord

Summer in Sweden   32

Skiing, Dog Sledding and Kiss a Moose   34

A Swedish Christmas   36

Icelandic Elves and Fishermen   39

Kurdish Refuge in Eastern Turkey   42

Mountains of the Moon, Uganda   50

Africa in the Mallee at Monarto Zoo   55

The Hidden Delights of a Smuggler's Port   60

Ships' Buoys in Valletta   63

Catherine Hamlin and the Fistula Hospital,
Ethiopia (1994)   72

Refugees in the Ogaden, Ethiopia (1994)   79

Baboon Encounter in the Fantale Crater,
Ethiopia (1996)   87

Fred Hollows and the Road to Axum,
Ethiopia (1997)   92

Lake Tana, Ethiopia (2000)   99

Tracking Predators in South Africa   105

Epilogue   109

Preface

There was a Moreton Bay fig tree at the bottom of our garden, and a treehouse was built by nailing wooden planks across its generous boughs under a leafy canopy. Here was a place to be away from the adult world, a haven of imagination, childhood secrets and dreams, the silence broken only by birds and the rustling of leaves.

I would lie back and study the clouds, with their ghost-like shapes forming and reforming, from a castle to an ogre, an elephant to a cherub, ephemeral, nebulous but with endless possibilities, like mirages. Mirages lure us to the next destination, only we find another one beaconing, and then another.

This collection of memoirs spans a 40-year compulsion to reach the next mirage, a quest to discover a little more of life and the wonders of nature, to gain understanding of the human condition.

Heather Caddick, 2015

Outback Cattle Drive Riding with Drovers

A rush of horses through the trees,
A sound of stock whips on the breeze
The drover's life has pleasures
That the townsfolk never know

BANJO PATERSON

City born and bred, but with my heart in the bush, I jump at the chance to join The Great Australian Outback Cattle Drive. Guests are invited to ride with the drovers, moving a mob of 500 cattle from Ooodnadatta to Maree. I choose the Lake Eyre sector. It will take five days.

Staging cattle drives was the brainchild of well-known South Australian bushman Keith Rasheed who, when chatting with mates some years ago, bemoaned the loss of the old cattle culture and the skills of droving, now replaced by motorbikes and road transport.

The first cattle drive in 2002 was followed, in 2005, by a well publicised drive that attracted worldwide interest. A large contingent of international guests and media attended, resulting in a tourism showcase for outback Australia.

There are 67 guest riders on our sector, skirting Lake Eyre South and traversing the immense Anna Creek station, the old Ghan railway line, and the 5400-kilometre dingo fence erected to divide cattle and sheep country and keep out dingoes.

My itinerant mountain-climbing son has arrived in Adelaide to reconnect with family, so the two of us will join the drive, setting off by plane to Roxby from Adelaide and then to Curdimurka, two hours by road from Roxby Downs. We fly over gorgeous country, bright with rich green patches and silvery creeks that carve the ochre red earth after recent rains. The water has not yet reached Lake Eyre South, a white and barren sea of salt, and an endless wave of deadly mirages.

We arrive at the cattle drive site to discover that this is not a rough and tough outback camp, but is cleverly fused with luxury. Young volunteers, dressed in monogrammed rugby shirts and Aussie Akubra hats greet us. Some are students from Adelaide and their friendliness and willing assistance creates a happy spirit in the camp. The campsite centre has a marquee that seats 100, including guests, drovers and crew, and a separate tented library contains books on flora, fauna and history, with maps of the region. Adjoining the marquee is a drinks van, shaded by colourful umbrellas with bar tables, and in the central square is the campfire site, a great place for a sundowner or three, and a yarn with drovers and Aboriginal elders after the day's ride.

The tents are carpeted, and bunk beds have cream sheets with chocolate-coloured doonas and comfy pillows. There are crisp white towels and a stand for clothes, with halogen lanterns for after dark, but this year I have remembered to bring my 'miner's light', a torchlight on a headband. The thoughtful organisers have provided earplugs to block the cacophony of snores from nearby tents, and prevent the temptation to take a cattle prod to offenders. We have been issued with bum bags for our day in the saddle, monogrammed with the cattle drive

logo, and containing a water bottle pouch, sunscreen, plastic raincoat and a liquorice treat for the horse.

Various Australian tourism bodies have been involved with the development of the cattle drive. I congratulate them for the brilliant concept of the shower and loo trailers, the clever use of space. Large mirrors, hand basins and hair dryers 100 kilometres from anywhere! The loo trailer has flushing toilets that would do Kenny proud; no long drops here!

We park our bags and change into jodhpurs, pick up our riding helmets and are bussed out to meet the drovers, strappers and our horses. Each guest has been matched with a horse from Anna Creek station, a vast property owned by the Kidman family, whose patriarch was Sydney Kidman, the 'Cattle King'. We are helped by Stewart Nunn, who recently retired as manager of Anna Creek, and Rodney, one of the chief drovers, who has worked there for 35 years.

Darryl Bell, known as 'the boss', his daughter Shannon and a fleet of young drovers will be our leaders and mentors for the drive. The Boss tells me he is 82 and has been a drover all of his life. Drovers and stockmen are the kings of the outback, with skills that leave us gasping in admiration. They ride as if fused to the saddle, using strength and courage to deal with breakouts, cracking stock whips with precision to round up stray beasts.

I am introduced to Wess, a 16-hand chestnut, and my horse for the drive. Step blocks allow for easy mounting, and strappers help and guide us through the yards. The cattle are released and Rodney instructs us to border the mob, walking at a gentle pace behind to allow the drovers to gallop, crack whips and direct the traffic.

This afternoon's introduction to droving allows us to get to know our horses and relax. We adjust to the sounds and smells of the mob and the fine red bull dust, and marvel at the intoxicating beauty of the country and the sense of freedom and space. The logistics of the drive are daunting. There are water troughs on trucks that move behind the mob, and lunch sites are set up each day for guests, with a small marquee housing a delicious smorgasbord, a campfire, and benches set up for the two-hour break before the afternoon drive, which ends around 5 pm. We dismount and take our horses to the water trough; they are given nose bags and corralled for the night.

We are bussed back to camp to use the shower trailers and meet at the campfire for a black rat (Bundy and Coke in a can), as we watch the slow setting sun streak the sky orange and red. Dinner is a feast of roasts, vegetables and salads, with sticky date or chocolate fudge pudding and ice cream to follow, all beautifully displayed and partnered with good wine. Guests of all ages, mostly Britons, New Zealanders and Americans, with local horsey people, cattlemen and city slickers like us, mix and match at the trestle tables. The atmosphere is inclusive and friendly, and drovers, volunteers, station owners and bush legends mingle and yarn with us all. After dinner, Reg, an Aboriginal elder from the Arabunna people, may play his guitar, or a group of drovers sing country music under arguably the clearest view of the Milky Way in Australia. Most guests are happy to sink under their doonas early, ready for a 6 am bugle call for breakfast and a 7.30 am departure. Breakfast is another feast, complete with the joy of brewed coffee or excellent tea.

By 8.30 am, Wess and I are riding with the mob, and not only do I feel part of the drive, but that I was born and bred to drove cattle. During the next three days we move through the ochre-red pebbles of the gibber country to Mulga scrublands and on to the Mallee. We slowly cover 14 kilometres a day. The mind fills with different priorities: cattle, horses and the terrain. There is time to talk, to listen and think, interspersed with adrenalin-stirring incidents.

The mountain man's horse is spooked by a water truck shuddering past, as we move the mob alongside the dirt road to Maree. The horse bucks in a classic Butch Cassidy mode, but he manages to stay in the saddle. Sue, from England, has to jump free when her mount decides to roll in the sand while crossing sand dunes. We watch, impressed, as she remounts, learning that horses will behave like naughty children if allowed. We see a drover gently carry a newborn calf to rest in a ute. The calf is later returned to its mother, strong enough to walk with the mob.

It is a privilege to ride alongside 'the boss'. He looks the part, with a stock whip draped around his shoulder, his moulded bush hat, and his stories coloured with wit and philosophy, gleaned from generations of droughts and floods and the highs and lows of a hard-fought life I doubt he would swap with anyone on earth.

This passion affects us all. On our final night at camp, a fireworks display competes briefly with the heavenly display above, and I notice my mountain man son is sounding more like a desert plains cattle man, and the cattle drive has gently but permanently branded us to the outback, and to the rich culture of Australian drovers.

For the Love of Rhinos

'For an actress to be a success, she must have the face of Venus, the brains of Minerva, the figure of Juno, and the hide of a rhinoceros'

ETHEL BARRYMORE

With further investigation, Ethel would have discovered rhinos respond to companionship, are curious and playful, and gravitate towards children.

They can be traced back to the Jurassic period and are happy to wander solo in the wild, or in small family groups, becoming aggressive only if their territory or family hierarchy is threatened.

The southern white rhino was a leading target for big game hunters a century ago. Photos of luminaries, like Hemingway, his foot on the carcass of a slaughtered rhino, gun in hand and a look of triumph on his face, are the thankfully now dated badge of honour of macho-man's triumph over danger. The slaughter emptied Africa of white rhino and by 1910, when only 100 remained, a concerted conservation program was initiated to prevent this extraordinary animal's extinction. Today there are thriving populations in protected reserves around the world. Monarto Zoo's involvement with the white rhino breeding program began in 2002, when seven white rhinos were imported to the zoo from Kruger National Park, South Africa, to boost the genetic pool of white rhinos in the Australasian region.

I have been invited to join colleagues from Wildlife Veterinary Operations, Kruger Research Centre, to take part in a white rhino capture in the reserve. I am staying in the veterinary camp at the Centre and, on being woken at 5 am, stagger to the camp kitchen for coffee and Afrikaner sweet rusks. Then, it's a kit check for camera, binoculars and hat, and jumping into the four-wheel drive. We stop at the security gate to allow a big tusker to saunter past. He barely gives us a glance as he slowly selects choice foliage with his trunk.

Sunrise lights the sky as we drive to the airport, where a National Parks helicopter is being checked over for our departure. On board are the pilot, two vets and one marksman (who will dart the selected rhinos from the helicopter). I join them as a privileged observer. This is a smooth and professional operation; the care and welfare of animals is the top priority in this military precision exercise.

South African National Parks hold three rhino auctions a year, offering around 200 rhinos for sale. Potential buyers are vetted and must be registered as suitable buyers. (The price for a male white rhino was around AU$60,000 in 2010.) The money raised supports the conservation and research of the white rhinoceros. Today, we need to capture two male rhinos for an auction to be held in Pretoria.

We take off, and the magnificence of the vast Kruger Reserve spans the horizon. We are flying low over the veldt, and it is possible to spot a jackal darting across a riverbed, elephant bathing in a waterhole and giraffe striding through the trees near a cluster of kudu. We are heading towards the eastern border of Kruger, where the rhinos will be selected. Poaching has increased alarmingly in this area, so the presence of the

capture team and the helicopter will be an extra deterrent to poachers. Kruger Reserve is the size of Wales, and patrolling anti-poaching squads are constantly challenged.

Between 2000 and 2007, 120 rhinos were poached from Kruger. In the 18 months before this trip, the figure has doubled. Rhinos are poached for their horns, the contraband travelling through Singapore to Vietnam and China to satisfy the demand for so-called miracle cures for everything from cancer to HIV/AIDS, as well as for its supposed aphrodisiac qualities. The most sinister of all is the popularity of a new health drink boasting two grams of ground rhino horn. As a result, the horns command a huge bounty and to impoverished African communities near the Reserve, the rich rewards are worth the risk.

A magnificent male rhino is spotted and we fly to the waiting transport truck and the on-ground vet team. We land and join the team while the pilot takes off with the marksman in a harness strapped to the side of the helicopter. They fly over the rhino, herding him toward the ground team. He is expertly darted. The sedative is finely tuned to allow the animal a speedy revival, and the team the opportunity to walk him gently to the transport truck. In earlier times, a stronger sedative would completely knock out the animal, which can weigh up to 2800 kilograms. It would then be lifted by crane on to the transport.

The operation works like clockwork, and the darted rhino walks towards the track, staggers a little and then lies down. Five vets simultaneously conduct medical checks, including taking blood and faeces samples, and then tag the rhino. It is not long before the sedative weakens and he begins to revive. The vets are then helped by a group of 20 keepers and Park's employees to get him back onto his feet. He is then carefully blindfolded and secured with ropes and, with the team pulling and guiding him, he walks slowly to the transport and up the ramp to be settled inside. He will be driven to the boma at Skukuza research camp. This operation is repeated when another male rhino is selected, and with the same degree of accuracy and precision he is safely secured for transport to the boma.

There are now 10,000 white rhinos in Kruger as a result of successful breeding over the past few years, but this is countered by poaching, and the human population demanding more land from the wild. Conservation work is always under threat. Eco-tourism is emerging as a growth area, providing opportunities for local communities to make a living other than from subsistence farming, and creating a chance for conservation to develop and to preserve what is left of the wild. The ideal would be to allow a balance to exist between human life and wildlife.

Postscript

This adventure with the veterinary wildlife operations took place in 2010. Three years on the poaching and mutilation of these gentle giants of the wild has increased to such an extent, that in April 2013 rhino poaching was cited as a national disaster in South Africa, making the problem eligible for government disaster funding.

Overwhelmingly it is a problem of education. Rhino horn is made of keratin (like the human fingernail) and is devoid of health benefits. In 2013, the demand for shark-fin soup in China dropped by half after a successful education campaign using social media, and I feel a flicker of hope for rhinos.

There are strong moves to decriminalise rhino poaching if the poachers harvest the rhino horn by cutting it, but leave the rhino unharmed. Trade in rhino horn could be controlled rather like the diamond trade in South Africa.

In December 2013, The Australian Rhino Project was established, aiming to bring 100 rhinos to Australia within the next two years, to establish an insurance population of rhinos in a safe haven. This, coupled with strong education programs directed at South-East Asia and China through social media, will hopefully bring rhinos back from the brink of extinction.

The Relevance of Zoos Today

'History is a race between education and catastrophe'

H.G. WELLS

The term climate change is misleading; the world's climate has always changed. What is different this time is the explosion of the world's population with its blind pursuit of life's comforts disrupting the fragile balance of our planet. This is creating a climatic disorder, where droughts, violent storms and rising sea levels are impacting on human life.

Floating around the northern Pacific Ocean is a mass of plastic the size of the United States of America. The ocean floor is being sprinkled with plastic grains that never disintegrate and are ingested by fish. We have slashed and burnt forests, replacing them with cultivation and urbanisation. We have dammed and diverted river systems, killed inland seas, and pillaged the oceans of fish and sea life. Cities are clogged with a cocktail of emissions from cars and factories, the night sky a dull mass and the sparkling firmament a distant memory. Frogs are disappearing, as are bees; consider the catastrophe of their total absence to our wetlands and the lack of pollination of our crops.

We have in a short time created a climate disorder, by completely disregarding the natural balance of life between plants, the ocean and the atmosphere. We are supposedly the most talented species on the planet, able to make a bionic arm, replace a heart, explore space, and design a baby. But somehow we seem to be ignoring the signs of stress in our environment.

Political debate seems to overtake the problems by sidelining confrontation and putting off direct action. Although we might rate ourselves as the most intelligent and innovative species, we are upstaged by the animal world in its capacity to evolve and adapt to change.

Wildlife that is absent from human meddling evolves in a miraculous way, adjusting to changed conditions in order to survive. Giant pandas can swivel their wrists to deftly handle bamboo and this physical attribute evolved as they became more reliant on bamboo as their staple diet.

Cheetah have dark pigmentation under their eyes to reduce the glare of the sun as they hunt by day. Giraffes have a 45 centimetre tongue to wind around branches and draw foliage into their mouths. Kangaroo can hold a foetus in diapause during a drought and the foetus will continue to develop after the drought is over.

So it is not surprising that wildlife captures our interest and curiosity, and surveys done of zoos worldwide show that people want to see wild animals, and make a connection to the natural world.

In Australia there are 15 million zoo visits each year. This figure doubles organised sport and other leisure activities. So we have a captive audience of large visitor numbers who want to make a connection with wildlife and who want to share this experience with their children and grandchildren.

If we can make zoo visits memorable, and allow close contact with the animals in our care, we can hopefully trigger an emotional connection with wildlife that should encourage people to lead a greener lifestyle, and join the cause for repairing our damaged planet.

Around 70,000 students spend class time at Adelaide and Monarto Zoos every year, and coupled with a dramatic rise in visitor numbers, there is a groundswell of potential wildlife protectors. If zoos worldwide can transmit a message of hope for wildlife, maybe this could trigger action to stop the destruction of wild habitats, and a tipping point could be reached to restore a balance between human life and wildlife, helping to calm the climate disorder.

Annapurna Trek

'Culture is the expression of a nation's character, and at the same time a powerful instrument to mould character'

SOMERSET MAUGHAM

We are sheltering in a village teahouse with no chimney, smoke from the central fireplace fills the room before escaping through the slits in the wooden slatted walls. We have trekked for seven days in the Nepalese Himalaya, attempting the Annapurna circuit, but a freak storm with heavy clouds and slippery rocks prompts Lopsang, our Sherpa guide, to seek refuge with villagers for the night.

They live perched on a grassy knoll in a cluster of wooden huts around a mountain stream. Here cows meander, goats wander, and chooks scavenge but scatter when village children run by. This seems a friendly haven of rural life, 12000 feet above the sea, and dwarfed by the 26,000 feet of Himalayan peaks.

The village chief welcomes us. We are warmly invited to a dinner and bunk space for the night, a change from our little tents and welcome protection from the sudden drop in temperature. Sherpa mountain men are formidable in physical strength, belying their slight frames, and they have a proud dignity reflecting their cultural background and courageous history. There is a mischievous humour in their smiles, masking a wisdom that seems innate to all those who live in wild regions, subject to the whims of the elements. We have been quick to

accept their sound mountain knowledge, and to adopt their health remedies.

When eight-year-old Barney suffered nausea and dizziness from the high altitude, Lopsang deftly wound a bandana into a headband, tying it firmly across his temples to create pressure. He then gently lifted him to his shoulders for a piggyback ride as we continued along the trail, and within half an hour the bandana was removed and Barney's symptoms had gone.

There is a squawk behind the inn as a chook is beheaded for the planned dinner feast, and village women appear bearing cauldrons of rice and curd, which are ceremoniously placed on the fireplace coals. Heavy woven rugs are brought to wrap over our inadequate trekking gear; the temperature has now dropped to freezing point. The atmosphere is charged with animated chatter among the locals, punctuated with jokes and laughter. Cards and backgammon are being played by the light from yak butter candles, and the smoke-filled room is woven with spicy cooking steam wafting from cauldrons.

Sherpas treat the porters as a lower caste. Their days are long and hard with low pay supplemented by free meals and the possibility of a tip from Western trekkers. Their glazed eyes and calm demeanour has probably more to do with the wild cannabis plants growing along the trail than Zen Buddhism. They carry huge loads up the steep mountain tracks. Some of the porters have no shoes, and yet they deftly jump from rock to rock with a 60-kilogram load balanced across their shoulders, saucepans and frypans dangling to the side and clanging together with each jump, their handles linked by rope. One porter carries a cast-iron primus stove, others take the tents and bedding. It is a human caravan that snakes along the trails,

and they magically construct a welcoming campsite each night.

The snowstorm and this village haven has given the porters a rare night off, so they gather together to smoke and gossip in a stable area behind the inn.

Over dinner we listen to Lopsang's yeti stories, and the encounters, footprints, and shadows of Nepal's abominable snowman become surreal in the smoky candlelight. Every local seems to own a yeti story, and like the Loch Ness monster, the fable is embellished and individualised, so that showing disbelief or scepticism would be heretic. We finally climb into our sleeping bags, along the wooden benches, fully clothed, complete with parkas, beanies, gloves and balaclavas. It is bitterly cold and the snow powders through the wooden slats making striped patterns that sparkle, and my breath freezes into an ice block across my balaclava. The wind is now a howling gale and the hut creaks against its force, but we are protected even if I find sleep impossible. I do notice that our two boys are fast asleep. Before long the wind drops and the silence is broken by robust snoring from all directions.

Hours later, as light finally breaks through the slatted planks, I stand up with my sleeping bag still zipped high, find the bottom of the bag, locking one foot into each corner, and shuffle my way outside. It feels like I have entered the Kingdom of Heaven, with pink dawn light revealing blue skies, clear and still, and air crisp as crystal. It is not as cold, now the bitter wind has dropped. The snow-covered peaks are streaked with pink, and I feel as if I am in arm's reach of touching them. The sheer size and ethereal beauty of this place is almost beyond description, and puts our human existence into perspective.

In the morning light our grassy-knoll village and teahouse

inn is revealed to be an ancient agrarian terrace, balancing on a precipice that falls further than I dare look down. These terrace communities cluster along the trekkers' trails, and for centuries this trail was a trading route and part of the Silk Road connecting China with India.

Our memorable night with the locals has been a replay of centuries of hospitality extended to travellers and traders who lead their pack mules and yak caravans through these formidable mountain passes. The centuries of swapping stories and embroidering catastrophes have nurtured mountain folklore, and help this culture thrive today.

I am jolted away from my philosophical musing by the village activity around the teahouse and the seductive smells: bread dough cooking in the cast-iron oven, porridge, and sweet tea brewing. There is a shedding and folding of sleeping bags, and hot water poured into tin basins for washing. I wind a clean cotton scarf around my head and after a face scrub and donning a fresh T-shirt, I'm done. Alfie and the boys are already dressed, with backpacks stacked and ready waiting near the porters assembling their kits.

Breakfast is served in the morning sunlight and, having survived the storm together, we are feeling part of this village community. There is laughter and teasing and hooning around, until Lopsang assembles his group of human foot-sloggers, and we loop into our backpacks and prepare to set off. The porters seem refreshed and buoyant, and the local villagers energised after our visit. We are eager, curious to see what lies ahead, but more than this we realise we have experienced a remarkable insight into different lives, lived with humour and kindness, within this extraordinary and unpredictable mountain range.

Soweto by Tuk Tuk

'Freedom is the last and best hope on earth'

ABRAHAM LINCOLN

A heat haze hovers over Soweto and the cloudless sky and glaring sun has families clustering under trees or lying on lush grass nearby. The silence is broken by the delighted shrieks of children dressed in vivid colours and braided mop-tops or peaked caps on the playground swings. Abstract African art is graffitied on the wall of the playing field, and to the east the ground rises to the railway line that links Soweto to Johannesburg.

Soweto is an abbreviation for South Western Townships, and was established in 1886 to house the black labour force for the gold mines in Johannesburg. In 1976 the South African police opened fire on black teenagers protesting in Soweto in response to the cruel apartheid regime in South Africa. The international outcry fuelled Soweto's anti-apartheid activists. After a long struggle, Nelson Mandela became the first black president of South Africa in the multi-racial elections held in 1994.

Dudu was born in Soweto and is a fine example of the post-apartheid generation, achieving tertiary education and majoring in tourism. She now manages the successful Soweto Tuk Tuk Tours. Dudu is petite, generous and funny. She relishes the freedom her parents were denied, loves Soweto with a passion, and wants to show tourists something of the excitement of Soweto today.

A daffodil yellow tuk tuk, scattered with floral art and love slogans is waiting by the park, a return to 1970s flower power. Lebo is at the wheel and we set off with the high-pitched engine, flowery decor and love slogans ensuring a positive reaction from passers-by. It is Saturday, so we head for the street markets.

Bright red and white striped awnings shade luscious fruit stalls, and bustling vendors sashay between shoppers, with higgledy-piggledy rows of chairs and tables, enticing us to pause for a coffee. A shebeen nearby is the mecca to locals for home brew, but we settle for shade and a strong coffee.

Nearby Miriam, in magenta silk cinched with a diamond buckle under an ample bosom, shades granddaughter Abigail with a flowered parasol. Friendliness tinged with curiosity results in merging our tables, and I hear about her love of choir singing for the Soweto Gospel Choir, and her pride in Abigail's progress at Letisbogo high school.

We climb back into our tuk tuk and head for the extraordinary $18 million Soweto Theatre Complex, completed in 2012 as part of Johannesburg's redevelopment plan for Soweto. We marvel at its size, contemporary design, and the prime colours reminiscent of a giant Legoland. Stagehands are unloading props for an upcoming performance.

During apartheid, theatre companies were formed by actor-activists, inspiring and encouraging South Africans to defeat apartheid by staging powerful works on the horrors of racist rule. Today they use the performing arts to inspire the fight against crime, violence and corruption.

We tootle back to visit the Nelson Mandela Museum and notice queues snaking round corners from the entrance.

Opposite the museum is a pub, and shady trees shroud the terrace, so we decide to have tea and gooey cakes in the shade to wait out the queues.

Nearby robust Afrikaans rugby types are chilling out after today's game at the World Cup Stadium, a monolith built in Soweto for the FIFA cup of 2010. The atmosphere here is friendly and inclusive, and supporters display their teams on scarves and T-shirts. Across the road we share Mandela adoration as we finally wander through the museum among the multi-cultural visitors, here on a pilgrimage to learn more about South Africa's father of freedom.

It has been a day of wonderful surprises, a chance to glimpse into Soweto's soul.

Middle East Hijinks and Hijacks

*'God protects drunks, infants and spirited girls who
are ready for anything'*

ANON.

Jules left husband number one for a Norwegian Adonis, her lifestyle now the glamour of an expatriate living in exotic places like Cyprus and Beirut. With another move, this time to Athens, she quickly found a job guiding wealthy American Jews to the Holy Land. The tours began with a week in Egypt cruising the Nile, followed by a week in Israel. The Adonis was managing an airline company in Athens, and their lives were in a state of perpetual motion, with all the luxuries and delights that go with entertaining clients or, in Jules's case, showing grateful and passionate Jews around Israel.

She still had family in Adelaide and would visit them from time to time, and when we met, I was knee-deep in footy sox, parent meetings and career challenges – not to mention a large house to clean and two Dobermans to be walked. This was a different era, and my bloke ('the disciple') felt that watering the garden was a fair contribution to family admin, although I will acknowledge he was a wonderful father and loved to read stories and play sports with our two boys. When Jules and I discussed and compared our lives, she suggested I join her on one of her Middle Eastern tours, as a breather from domesticity.

'All you need do is book airfares,' she said, 'and you can join me as a trainee tour guide. I always have a double room and so accommodation will be free. The company in Athens will never know, and hotels don't count travel group numbers at breakfast, so if you fly to Cairo, I shall give you my room number, and you won't need to check in.'

How deliciously naughty, I thought, and what a way to launch my 40th year. So I jumped at the chance, and arrangements were negotiated gently, bolstered by the knowledge that much-loved grandparents lived close by, ready to ease any strain on the disciple.

I leave in June 1985. The heat from the tarmac assaults passengers as we disembark in Cairo and jam ourselves into a waiting bus to weave through a maze of planes and trucks to the terminal. Security is extreme after a decade of plane hijackings in Europe and the Middle East. These attacks are politically motivated by Moslem terrorists who have commandeered planes in flight. Sometimes planes have been grounded on a runway, with passengers held hostage and ransom demands made to their national governments. It is a courageous time to travel in the Middle East.

I notice that the customs and immigration queue in the Cairo arrivals hall is moving at a snail's pace. Every item of luggage is checked. The atmosphere is tense. Airport terminals in the region have also been recent terrorist targets. I scrutinise the crowds, trying to detect suspicious-looking characters who could be terrorists in disguise, but it is not easy as most men are swathed in Arab scarves and are wearing dishdashas, so I decide to ease the tension by playing the dumb chatty blonde, as the officials delve into my case and toss lacy lingerie across the customs desk. I make a glib comment about dangerous underwear and start giggling. This sets off other passengers in

the queue, who fish out jocks and bras for inspection. Decorum is restored when a rotund and officious manager marches over to see what is going on, and so we quickly seal our smiles and return to serious compliance. Finally my case is ticked, and I am free to find a taxi and head for the hotel.

The hot and pungent air blows through the window and my legs are sticking to the car seat, cream linen bermudas and blouse pasted to my skin, as the taxi driver regales me with a guided tour of Cairo. I am hoping he might slow down because the arrow is pointing to 80 mph on the dial. The highway from the airport is like a speedway with macho showing off and aggressive driving. My driver seems to relish the rivalry, his monologue boosted by each overtaking. He keeps one eye on the rear-vision mirror to see I remain his attentive audience.

I mention my father, based in Cairo during WWII before transfer to Palestine, and this unleashes a tirade of delight about Australian soldiers and their bravery during the war, and how much they are respected by Egyptians. We draw up to the kerb and he gets out of his cab to open the door for me.

'This trip is a present from my country to you, as an Australian,' he says. I have a little gold kangaroo pin in my bag, and pin it on his jacket. He bows, smiles and then bows again before driving away.

The hotel foyer is busy and I see a blonde curly mop head in the middle of a group of wealthy-looking Americans. There is monogrammed luggage in mounds to the side, with eager porters standing by. Jules sees me and we hug in delight, relieved that we've met without a hitch. I am introduced to the group as Heather, our trainee tour guide from Australia. Amazingly, there is no comment, just polite and friendly greetings. It is easy to blend in with the tour group as rooms are allocated, and finally we get to our room. Jules says that we must make my bed perfectly in the morning so staff believe there was only one occupant in the room.

There is a knock at the door and the announcement: 'House keeping!' I dive into the wardrobe, with a clatter of coathangers as I close the door, and Jules lets the maid in to check the mini bar and turn down her bed. She departs and I climb out of the cupboard amid stifled giggles, and we spend the evening catching up on news.

It appears the Adonis now has a Greek rival in Athens, Cristos by name and, as he has phoned Jules three times already, I am guessing he could be a tad possessive and not happy that his new love is jaunting around the Middle East. He asks us to buy two ghetto-blasters, now the latest in hi-tech equipment, as they are far cheaper in Cairo. He will meet us at the runway steps on our return, so as to avoid customs in Athens. I am finding that things are done rather differently in this part of the world, and sense that Cristos must have some influential friends in Athens.

We finally sleep, and in the morning I practically iron the bedspread in an effort to make the bed look unused. We go down together for breakfast, a buffet of fruit, pastries and coffee, and a chance to get to know the group. I notice that chiffon dresses, opulent trouser suits plus jewellery seems to be the dress code. Even the men, no doubt dressed by their spouses, are wearing formal shirts and conservative jackets.

'Don't they know the climate here?' I say to Jules.

'They are first timers,' she says, 'and the Nile cruise is marketed as glamorous, so they are dressing for a luxury cruise.'

We meet in the foyer for a transfer to the airport for the flight to Luxor, where we shall board the ship for a five-day cruise to Aswan. As the flight leaves from the domestic terminal, the atmosphere relaxes, and soon we are taking off through the morning mist to the clear azure sky above. The cockpit door is open, and I can see the captain flirting with a crew hostess as she draws seductively on a cigarette, a glorious smile as she exhales. I am hoping his focus might return to the instrument panel and our destination, but mercifully this is short flight and soon we are taxiing to the Luxor terminal.

The *Isis Dream* is moored in a line of at least ten cruise ships along the Nile bank in Luxor. We have spent the morning in Karnak, two kilometres from Luxor and the site of the enormous and ancient temple of the Pharaohs, replete with ram-headed sphinxes, columns inscribed with hieroglyphics and obelisks. A renowned professor from Cairo University is our guide and after two hours of nonstop verbiage, despite its brilliance, with the dust, 40°C heat, and a mob of vendors in our wake, our ship is a welcome sight. Our polite Americans are flagging, shedding their jackets and as many other items of clothing as prudently as possible, and are gasping for the *Isis Dream* to relax and cool off.

There is a commotion beside the gangway with shouting and animated discussion between ship's staff and what look like tradesmen. The ship's air conditioning has broken down, but will be fixed soon they say, and we are to board and check in to our cabins. It feels like a sauna inside, and apologetic staff serve iced pomegranate juice as we mill around reception. Humour is the only response, I think, to placate our travellers, who are tired and streaming with sweat amid rumblings of discontent.

We gather them together to discuss shopping at the bazaars, which tempers the mood, and we promise we shall take them to the best jewellery outlets before we sail tonight. They trundle off to their cabins to unpack and rest.

Jules and I find our cabin and open the porthole to let in the hot breeze, an improvement on unpacking in a stifling shoebox. The intercom crackles and a relieved voice announces that the cool air system is now working and a loud purring can be heard in the ceiling vents of our cabin. This is promising. The shower works and suddenly all is right with the world, except Jules is fielding cabin calls from our group … what shall I wear? What time is dinner? Do you have a headache cure? Where do we change money? Can we drink the water? She is running all over the ship tending to their problems, whilst the 'trainee guide' is taking a siesta before leading these lambs into the arms of the bazaar traders.

The evening call to prayer resounds over the river and the blood-red sun is sinking. It casts pink auras into a fading blue sky. The noise on the river banks is in crescendo as Luxor awakens after the daytime heat. People promenade along the corniche, families grouping under trees with picnic baskets placed on colourful rugs, children shouting as they play together, and street vendors plying their wares. The atmosphere is spiced with aromas from food stalls that dot the walkways. The bazaar entices all visitors. Jules has clients who own stalls here and compete for her travel groups, as she is a regular visitor and there are good profits to be made.

Female rivalry within our group is on display at Mohammed's Jewels and Artifacts. Coral and lapis lazuli necklets are haggled over and eventually bought. We intervene and suggest a lower

price to Mohammed if payment is made in US dollars, and of course he agrees because there is a buoyant black market in currency exchange, with the US dollar rising against the Egyptian pound every day.

We walk back to the *Isis Dream*. At dinner, necks are festooned with coral and lapis and worn over brocades and silks. A delightful Afro-American family is part of our group, the only non Jews. They live in New Jersey where Bill is an academic and Nina a teacher, and their teenage daughters have taken time out from school to join their parents. They seem to be somewhat isolated, not included in conversation. There is not the slightest effort from other tour members to extend a friendly hand. I suggest to Jules that we ask if we can join their table for dinner, and on doing so am appalled to hear Nina say, 'Oh, dear Heather and Jules, you don't have to do that!' We say we would be delighted to join them, and there begins a friendship that has lasted to this day.

The cruise wends its way up the Nile, the pool deck mandatory to cool off in the heat of the day – it would be insane to be inside and miss seeing life on the Nile banks as we drift by. The deep luscious green of the palms and exotic plants is broken by flowering trees, and donkeys laden with produce for local markets are hurried along by impatient vendors. A camel train meanders along the riverside track and feluccas sail by, their distinctive white sails a geometric delight against the blue sky. They are manned by Nubian fishermen, who have been fishing here almost since time began.

There are more ruins and temples to visit by day, and relaxed dinners with belly dancing, dress-ups, and charades on board at night. We finally arrive in Aswan where we reluctantly leave

the *Isis Dream* to fly to Cairo. We shall spend a night there before the Israeli chapter begins.

Ahmed, a travel agent in Cairo, has promised to meet Jules and me at the airport for a private transfer to the hotel. The group have been taken by bus to the hotel for a free night to relax before the early morning flight to Tel Aviv, so we feel an element of freedom from our charges as we meet Ahmed in the terminal. He reminds me of Omar Sharif, but with a more relaxed temperament as he scoops us up and we drive away in a silver four-wheel drive, again at eye-watering speeds along the freeway. There is no point in protesting, and I can see that our curly mop head has another fan. Jules accepts his dinner invitation, whereas I am happy to collapse in our hotel room for some blissful solitude.

Peace is a pipe dream, because Cristos phones from Athens every half hour to speak with Jules and barrages me with questions: Where is she? What is she doing? Who is she with? By the 11 pm phone call, my excuse of 'She's shopping with the tour group' sounds a bit hollow, so I phone reception, pretending to be Jules, and say they are not to put through any more calls from Athens. It is a man's world in Egypt, as it is in Greece, so more calls *are* put through. I finally tell Cristos to get lost, and leave the receiver off the hook, as the door opens and in she comes, saying the dinner was delightful!

I was unable to book the same flight as the group to Tel Aviv. The Israeli airline El Al has a segregated space at Cairo airport with armed guards standing around the plane in warrior pose, their guns aimed at chest height. On every El Al flight there are two Mossad officers seated amongst the passengers, so although boarding is scary, once seated I feel safe.

We arrive in Tel Aviv late at night. I am armed with a hotel name and room number. There is a sea of people, noise and general chaos at immigration, taking an hour to clear, and I don't relish the idea of a lone 60-kilometre taxi ride to Jerusalem. An elderly couple, hearing my dismay at the distance, offer me a ride with them, which I accept with delight and relief. Their driver is waiting outside beside a luxurious black Mercedes. I sink into the plush leather and notice a full moon casting light above the headlights as the driver smoothly accelerates along the highway to Jerusalem. Jakob and Elsa have lived in Jerusalem since 1950 and have children and grandchildren living close by. I ask them if they think these current horrors of terrorism could have been avoided with a fairer approach to the Palestinians, but get the impression that they believe Jews had a God-given right to take over Palestine. So I agree with them, as I have accepted their kindness, and wish them well with profuse thanks at the hotel.

It is now midnight, and the doors are locked, so I ring the buzzer and a night porter sleepily approaches. It is time for some feminine vulnerability; I confess about missing a flight with my travel group, and he lets me in. Fortunately the reception desk is unmanned, so I head for the lift and finally thump on the door of room 380 to wake Jules, who hugs me with relief. 'Thank heavens,' she says, 'you made it!'

Our time in Israel is a whirl of activity, with the Jewish group living their Holy Grail in the Holy Land with whispered reverence and wide-eyed acceptance of everything they are told by guides. After yet another holy site, accompanied by endless verbiage, I escape in Bethlehem to the Arab quarter, and go into a shoe shop to have my leather sandal repaired. I spend the morning with a Palestinian family, drinking tea and hearing their story of how things have changed, how they really are considered the dangerous underclass in Israel, with few options to improve their lot. There is wisdom and humour wound through their stories, with insights into generations of multi-religion friendships that are difficult to maintain in these political times.

Jerusalem has a beauty beyond description, and is superbly pristine and well maintained. There are markets in every square and robust commerce bleeds the tourist pilgrimage at every quarter. Hands are out and tins rattling for money at myriad religious sites. We spend a day at the Dead Sea and, bikini clad, we effortlessly float in the salted water as Israeli fighter jets buzz overhead.

Our travel group is now sated, laden with mementos to take back to New York as we prepare to leave Israel. Jules is nervous that I may not have the right papers to clear immigration on departure, as she has a group clearance and I am not on her list. We share an airport trolley, and in her rush to alert me, she trips over the front wheel, which overturns, causing an element of chaos. The armed guards scrutinise us. I start talking about how terrifying security is, and how I am from Australia and not used to all this tension, while Jules talks about trainee guides and how wonderful our trip has been to Israel. Somehow we manage to get through.

I suddenly feel a strong grip on my arm, and think, My god, this is it! I turn to see a smiling security guard saying, 'I heard you were frightened, please allow me to guard you until you leave.' He takes me to a quiet lounge and we have coffee and talk together until the final call for my flight. When all the passengers are already seated, he walks me to the plane. As he leads

me to my seat next to Jules, he kisses me on both cheeks, bows and says, 'Bon voyage, madame.'

This is TWA, an American airline, and as we taxi out I say to Jules what a relief it is to be on an American airline after all the dramas in the Middle East. During the flight to Athens we sit and chat with the TWA crew, exchanging recent experiences, joking and laughing.

True to his word, Cristos is at the foot of the runway in Athens with a bunch of red roses as we disembark with our luggage and ghetto-blasters. We take a separate passage out that by-passes customs and immigration.

On 14 June 1985, TWA flight 847, carrying the crew we befriended, was hijacked by Hezbollah on a flight from Athens. They were demanding the release of 700 Shi'ite Muslims from custody in Israel. This terrifying intercontinental hijacking lasted two weeks, passengers were threatened, some were beaten, a US navy diver was killed and his body thrown onto the tarmac. After some of the demands were met, the remaining passengers were set free.

Swedish Smorgasbord

'Love more and all good will be yours'
SWEDISH PROVERB

Summer in Sweden

We are in Sweden for a family christening in the cloister gardens of Varnhem Abbey, established by the Cistercian Order from France in 1150 AD. In those days these gardens grew herbs and supplied potions and medical remedies for the monks; today they are a riot of colour with wildflowers and neat hedges tangled with budding creepers, birdsong and butterflies.

Varnhem Abbey is the final resting place for medieval Kings of Sweden, with names like Erik Eriksson, otherwise known as 'Lisp and Limp', King Knut, Inge the Elder, and Birger Jarl. The ancient bell tolls in its wood-shingled tower, denying the local community of sleep with its sonic boom engulfing the valley, each *dong* emphasising the Abbey's central role in Varnhem life. Our little princess seems undaunted by the sound, and smiles and giggles throughout the ceremony.

Summer in Sweden, with the extra hours of sunlight and warm mellow days, changes life and behaviour. Swedes make the most of every moment during this short reprieve from winter. They become hunters and gatherers, and we are walked through the woods at daybreak to pick blackcurrants,

blueberries and raspberries. But the real mission is to find the elusive kantarella. These mushrooms are pale yellow and spindly and have a delicate flavour when gently cooked in butter. They are so prized by Swedes that they are gathered in secrecy and stealth. We are told all Swedes will lie in response to one question: 'Where did you find the kantarellas?'

The perfect Swedish summer meal is fresh fish caught from the lake, served with kantarellas gathered from the woods, followed by sweet ripe blackcurrants and raspberries, freshly picked and baked in a pie.

A bridge forms a gateway to our friend's house in the country, and family tradition demands that we greet the troll as we cross the bridge. This troll has guarded the farm for generations, and he lives under the bridge, or so they say. Our son has a healthy respect for trolls, as years ago he decided to loudly curse the troll as he rode across the bridge on a mountain bike. He promptly fell off the bike – and the bridge – in a spectacular crash. I am interested to see that, as a father, he respectfully greets the troll as we drive across.

There is a delightful formality to Swedish social life. All occasions require toasts and announcements, so on arrival we are ushered to a garden terrace to be formally welcomed with the first toast. A lucid and eloquent reply is expected, so it is wise not to indulge too liberally in the mind-blowing aquavit, as these toasts to friends, countries, sporting heroes and random topics will punctuate the dinner and the entire evening. We depart more than slightly the worse for wear.

Swedes love their history, culture and traditions, and nowhere is this more apparent than the Tuesday evening concerts held on Skansen, one of Stockholm's 14 islands. Crowds queue all afternoon to take part in the program of songs that trace Swedish folklore over the centuries. Families gather to sing together led by Swedish celebrities and watched by members of the Swedish royal family. Television coverage tops the ratings all over Sweden, and it seems the entire country is proudly taking part in this celebration of summer and life.

Skiing, Dog Sledding and Kiss a Moose

'The north wind doth blow and we shall have snow', plays on my mind as we wait to board the overnight ski train from Gothenburg to Are, Sweden's ski resort 320 kilometres south of the Arctic Circle. Style queen Tilda, aged five, is in full ski kit, and Erik the elk dangles from three-year-old Emmy's backpack, stuffed with champagne, our sensible remedy for the long night ahead.

We find the six-bunk compartment comfortable. The girls take the top bunks, their parents select the middle and we 'grandies' opt for ground level. They have crisp white sheets, navy fleecy blankets and adjustable pillows. After a Moomintroll story and the gentle motion of the train, the girls are fast asleep. Armed with the champagne we find the restaurant car, welcomed by a pack of skiers already in après-ski mode.

Rail journeys in my nomadic past were more of an endurance than a pleasure, but this is comfortable and great fun. When we finally hit the bunks we sleep like logs until dawn. Then it's a breakfast of excellent coffee and cinnamon buns, and time to marvel at the Arctic landscape of iced lakes and fir forests heavy with snow.

We skirt Lake Storsjon, where a mythical monster rivalling

Loch Ness has fascinated locals for over 1000 years. The last paranormal encounter was documented in 2008. Today, however, all monster secrets remain hidden with the lake firmly iced over and sparkling pink in the morning light.

We arrive at Are station and thick snowflakes are feathering the sky, so it's a relief to have a covered walkway to our hotel, sitting at the lake's edge close to the town centre. It has been built to a Finnish concept, where indoor activities rival everything that the ski slopes have to offer. There is an enormous indoor swimming pool with islands, bridges and waterfalls, and a water slide weaving outside and in, spilling you into a hot plunge pool. Huge windows capture the iced lake, pinky aqua sky and snow peaks.

We head to the ski school, where Emmy joins the Snowballs class for three year olds, and it's all fun and games and high fives. Tilda, in her purple ski suit and scary orange helmet, masters the poma lift and disappears with her class. We are now free to ski the more challenging slopes of Are.

Mid week, we take a 'rest' day to dog sled in the Are hills. Each sled seats four, and we sit on deerskins with Sven, our driver, standing behind, controlling 12 huskies tethered in twos. He signals the lead dog and we set off at a cracking pace, racing along snow trails that wind through the woods and glades. There is a breathtaking feeling of freedom, and the exhilaration of being exposed to the elements, but safe with the huskies. Dog sledding was once the only way to get around in the wintry north and like our Aussie drovers has its own culture, legendary characters and proud history.

Our final adventure is with moose, considered to be the forest kings of Sweden, with the ancient moose hunt an annual

tradition embedded in Swedish folklore. Moose have distinctive antlers and a loveable dopey expression just begging for a kiss. So, we go to the Kiss a Moose farm and meet the moose, planting kisses on their velvety noses as our farewell to the wintry delights of Arctic Sweden.

A Swedish Christmas

Snow is falling in thick soft flakes that play with the light and silently transform our small town in country Sweden to the perfect Christmas postcard. We are pulling our little angels in sledges along a riverside trail, and they shriek with delight as they bump over mounds and dips and mad dog Magnus dive bombs snow drifts, more polar bear than giant schnauzer.

We come to the town square where every tree sparkles with fairy lights and an enormous Christmas tree presides in the centre. The air is scented with apple cinnamon from the cake stalls and hot mulled wine from copper tureens. Our little angels settle for hot chocolate, we choose the wine, and Magnus, now behaving, sits close by.

It is 12 December and the official launch of Christmas in Sweden. Ceremonies across the country celebrate Lucia, the Goddess of Light. Beautiful young girls in white girdled tunics wearing wreaths of lit candles on cascading blonde hair, walk slowly into the town square. After blessings from the town dignitaries, the church bell tolls and the Christmas celebrations can begin.

Trolls are still an active part of Swedish culture, and each house in the countryside has a troll's protection. Tomten, a

Christmas troll, wears red with a pixie hat and is full of mischief, but helpfully will watch and report on children's behaviour in the run up to Christmas.

We are spending Christmas at the summer house on a small lake at the edge of a forest. It looks like a gingerbread house iced in snow, with scarlet poinsettias and lit candles at each window and fairy lights studding the holly bushes at the front door. The lake has frozen over and a full moon lights the icy surface and casts beams through the trees.

The morning of Christmas Eve has the family assembled to walk through the woods and select the perfect Christmas tree. The procedure is punctuated by toasts, songs and rhymes. We toast the forest, we toast the trolls and finally we toast the chosen tree, which is then felled and carried back with great ceremony to the house for decoration.

An ancient sauna hut sits at the lake's edge, and has been belching smoke from its chimney stack for hours. We are about to indulge in the divine torture of a traditional Swedish sauna. It is ladies first and we sit together on trestled tiers, talking, laughing and slowly baking as eucalyptus water sizzles the fire. It is now time! Stark naked we jump from the sauna, and one by one roll in the snow with screams of horror from the Aussies and delight from the Swedes.

With a euphoric feeling of wellbeing we assemble back in the house to recover, helped by Christmas *gloegg*, a hot spiced wine, served with blanched almonds.

Our extreme sportsman son has been selected to wear the Santa suit. It is now early evening and the children crowd to the window watching for Santa's arrival. There are shouts of delight as they see him trudging up the path with a bulging red sack over his shoulders. He is welcomed with a toast of aquavit, or Swedish firewater, and he then sits by the Christmas tree announcing each child's name, before selecting a gift from the sack.

Soon it is time to toast Santa's farewell and then dinner is announced, a lavish Swedish smorgasbord of seafood, salads and good red wine. I have bought pavlovas, much to our family's delight, and later we weave our way along the forest trail to a little church for midnight mass with hopes and blessings for *god jul*. Merry Christmas.

Icelandic Elves and Fishermen

'Take notice of the past, if you want originality'
GRETTIR THE STRONG

In 14th-century Iceland, elves were often consulted before making a final judgement in regard to legal disputes. This strategy no doubt helped Grettir the Strong expand his empire and retain his strongman title as one of Iceland's Saga heroes. Today Icelanders belief in elves may be kept quiet, but it would be political suicide to claim they don't exist.

In 2012, amid a blaze of publicity, MP Arni Johnsen had a 50-tonne boulder moved from a busy highway to his front garden overlooking the sea. He claimed the elves who live inside the boulder had saved his life when his car crashed nearby, and as a reward they asked him to arrange a sea view for them.

Iceland's department of transport will delay or re-route road construction to avoid elf habitats, and they usually consult with elf spotters before finalising projects. Construction workers were instructed to carefully remove a large boulder on the new road to Reykjavik airport when spotters confirmed that it housed elves. Once the elf habitat had been relocated, they were relieved to find the frequent breakdowns of machinery and construction equipment ceased.

Whether Icelanders admit to their belief in elves or not, there is an undeniable sense of 'other worldness' in this stunningly beautiful and isolated island, where over the centuries earth-shattering volcanoes have drowned villages in lava,

Atlantic storms and tidal waves have swallowed fishing fleets, and thermal springs and bubbling volcanic lakes puncture the landscape.

Winter darkness shrouds the island, and wind, ice and snow means time spent indoors nurturing the rich heritage of storytelling.

When the banking bubble burst in 2008, Icelandic bankers shed their pin-striped suits and jumped back into their fishing boats. (A shrewd referendum allowed Iceland to default, letting the banks fail, and making foreign creditors and not Iceland's taxpayers cover the debt.) The free-fall devaluation of the krona, as a result of the default, kick-started the economy. Booming fish exports and jobs growth resulted – a very good reason for locals to relive their past lives through an industry that has sustained Iceland for generations.

Sigurmundur Einarsson has classic Viking looks, and his blond locks are tangled with sea salt. We are enjoying *fisksupa*, a delicious Icelandic fish chowder, at the harbour pub of Heimaey, a volcanic island off Iceland's southern coast. Heimaey was covered by lava during the 1973 volcanic eruption, and a Dunkirk-style rescue using fishing boats ferried 5300 residents to the mainland without one casualty. Once the lava cooled, a new village was built, and Heimaey now thrives as a fishing and tourism centre, a launch pad for tourists to track puffin colonies and whales.

Seas are temperamental here, and high velocity winds can see waves rise to 30 metres. Mercifully today is calm, and ex-banker Sigurmundur leads us to his family fishing ketch to show us around the waterways. Hundreds of puffins are busy nesting on the cliff face, and others are skimming the sea looking for

fish. We see a killer whale breach nearby as we enter the womb of the island through sculptured caves carved from volcanic rock over thousands of years. We drift around the central cave, light playing with water ripples and refracting to the ceiling dome.

Sigurmundur takes out his saxophone to play the blues, and the hauntingly beautiful tones expand into the cave, with rich echoes returning to engulf us in sound. There is a surreal and emotional intensity to the music, as if nature and humanity are being melded together by his saxophone playing and he is slowly spinning an invisible thread around us that will bind us indelibly to the Sagas of Iceland.

Kurdish Refuge in Eastern Turkey

'A kind word warms a man through three winters'

KURDISH PROVERB

It is 1988. Ten weeks in Turkey may sound excessive, but we are between jobs and our boys have their long school holidays, so we decide to go adventuring, as Toad of Toad Hall would say. It will be a bare basics budget holiday with hostel accommodation, and we shall use buses and trains to get around. We mark the far east of Turkey bordering Russia and Iraq, and Van, the former capital of Armenia, as destinations.

The cheap hotel in Istanbul is run by a Turkish family, and although shabby, it is clean, and we are warmly welcomed. The boys are hugged and their cheeks are pinched, to their horror. Barney's red hair is a fascination to them, as is our nationality. We seem to be the only tourists among the hotel's usual guests of local business people.

Each morning the hotel family suggests exciting places for us to visit. The boys are delighted by the Basilica Cistern, in Sultanahmet Square, bringing back memories of James Bond in *From Russia with Love*. The Cisterns were built by Justinian I in the sixth century, and later used as water storage for Topkapi Palace by the Ottomans. Every sound echoes, even a whisper, among the muted shadows from the tall pillars that line this underground wonderland.

The Egyptian bazaar is our next destination, and generous samples of Turkish delight are offered at every stall. There are many concoctions: chewy, nutty, rose and coconut flavoured, jelly soft and rock hard. We intersperse these treats by breathing in the pungent smell of spices displayed in open sacks along the alleyways.

Another long walk through the back streets leads us back to the Grand Bazaar, and we explore carpet shops, perfume vendors, gold souks and artefact markets. Although we are obviously just 'tyre kickers' and not spending money, we are offered generous hospitality and tea at every stop by friendly Turkish traders. Pleading fatigue, we finally wind our way to the Cemberlitas Hamami, probably Istanbul's most famous Turkish bath, built during the Ottoman Empire in 1584 AD.

The spa pool lies beneath an ancient domed ceiling, complete with porthole-like skylights that send sunbeams to the water below. There are fountains around the walls that spew sulphuric water to marble catchment pools, and you can sit alongside and douche your body, or sit under a waterfall gushing from the mouth of a carved marble gargoyle.

The baths are segregated, and I strip down in a locker room and enter the scrub-down annex in a towelling robe. Women and girls of all ages are lying face down on marble slabs, being vigorously scrubbed by rotund and jovial bath attendants. They are assertive as they direct traffic, adding a touch of humour and a laugh. It is interesting to see how inhibited Western women gradually relax among this mass of female nudity; how they enjoy the camaraderie (what our indigenous people of Australia might call 'secret women's business'). Since Ottoman times, the hamam has been a meeting place for all generations; grannies, mothers and daughters coming together to talk, laugh and gossip as they bathe. I watch a woman in her sixties seated on a marble slab by a fountain gently sluice the waters over her ten-year-old granddaughter. They giggle together, obviously adoring each other's company.

I lie face down on a marble slab, and my bath attendant slaps and scrubs me with what feels like sandpaper. She laughs with delight at my protests and sloshes me with spa water from the fountain. I'm instructed to plunge into the sparkling pool, feeling as clean as a spring shower.

The disciple and boys have been in the male hamam. Dressed in our toweling robes we meet in the communal restroom after our baths to drink sweet apple tea and rest on comfy sofas. Our skin is now pink and glowing with health.

We dress warmly, protected against a cold December wind blowing off the Bosphorous, and head for a bank near the Galata Bridge. A fishing boat with striped awnings is set up with a grill at its stern to cook the freshly caught fish. The fillets are grilled in butter and placed into a crusty fresh roll with raw onion and a squeeze of lemon juice. We decide that this is the most delicious meal on earth.

It is time to venture east. Bus stations are humming with activity, as bus travel is still the cheapest and best way to traverse Turkey. Touts yell out prices to remote destinations, each trying to outdo the other with travel offers. Once a bus is filled, the driver appears from nowhere, cigarette in hand, and jumps into the driver's seat and takes off. We discover there seem to be no rules on the roads in Turkey. Speed is the ultimate goal, so we decide to rule out night bus travel for safety reasons, and trust in the luck of the stars – or St Christopher – that all will be well. The 1200-kilometre bus trip to Erzurum in far eastern Turkey will take two days along narrow roads.

We choose front seats in the bus, a mixed blessing as we witness terrifying near misses as our driver speeds along the road. As compensation we get a perfect view of the vast Turkish plain, just made for a galloping Genghis Khan and his Mongol hordes. Loud Turkish music blares from crackly speakers, and bright tassels and evil eye trinkets decorate the windscreen and flutter and jingle with every bump. All the passengers are Turks, most sleeping propped against each other. The boys focus on video games, and for once I am happy about this distraction on such a long road journey.

A bus crammed full of passengers passes us. Our driver decides this is a challenge to his virility and immediately increases speed to catch up and overtake the bus. We are now neck and neck, racing along the narrow road, with both drivers determined to win. We yell in protest and mention the children on board as he passes the bus and turns to us with a shrug of his shoulders and a smile.

We have an overnight stop, and mercifully a change of drivers, and finally arrive in Erzurum, the capital of eastern Anatolia. The Erzurum plateau sits 1800 metres above sea level within solid Byzantine city walls. An horizon of jagged mountain peaks pierce the skyline. Our little hostel is warm, and friendly staff seem amazed at our arrival here in winter.

We decide to travel the six kilometres to Palandoken, a mountain resort boasting the longest ski run in the world. The road is narrow, steep and icy, and our driver has no tyre chains to grip the road, but he insists we shall get there safely, and with a few more swerves and slides, we arrive at a deserted hotel. It is early December and the resort is closed.

There are snow banks at the side of the road, so the drive

back to Erzurum is managed without us sliding off the track and down the slope. Heavy snow falls all night and the next day and despite the blizzard we decide to press on to Van, the former capital of Armenia. There is a frightening lack of visibility, but the driver seems confident that all is well, and the disciple checks that the bus has snow chains on the tyres. The passengers are local farmers and women. They have bought produce in Erzurum and will be dropped at their villages along the road to Van. The bus smells of cured meats and there are packages bulging with vegetables and fresh bread. Our boys seem to be the focus of admiration and much affection. Morsels of food are handed to them with the insistence they eat up. Turkish music is blaring and Toby is perched on a veiled granny's knee, being offered Turkish delight.

Van lies on the shores of Lake Van, and has been an urban centre since 5000 BC. Lake Van's beautiful Akdamar Island displays the elegant Armenian Cathedral of the Holy Cross, built 2000 years ago. Legend, myth and folklore maintain the lake is enchanted and often visited by angels. No angels protected the Armenians from the violence and horror of genocide that started in 1915 and ended their empire. Or the seizure of Armenia by Turkey. Since then a Kurdish majority has made Van their home.

The blizzard continues, and we are snowed in for three days. Record falls close all roads, rail lines and any communication to nearby villages. It is minus 15°C, and we spend each day meeting with Kurds, in carpet shops and small inns, drinking tea, and watching soccer on ancient TV screens that seem to snow as much as the snow falling outside. It is a siege mentality of fun and laughter, huddled indoors, eating hearty pea and ham soup by roaring fires, and experiencing unbelievable hospitality – coupled with amazement that an Australian family would choose to visit Van in winter.

We hear horrifying stories of Kurdish treatment at the hands of Saddam Hussein, just over the border in Iraq, and discover that there are many refugees from Iraq being cared for in this town. The news of chemical gas being used on the Kurds of Halabja, accompanied by appalling images, is discussed. The Kurds here are united by a determination to protect and care for any Iraqi Kurds who manage to escape.

The snowstorm has passed and rail lines and roadways are cleared, marking the end of our siege in Van. We choose a new-looking bus for our next journey, along the Turkish border with Iraqi and Syria to Diyarbakir. We need to climb out of the Van plateau and across a mountain range before heading south.

We leave early afternoon, and the disciple notices there are no snow chains on the bus tyres, but assumes they have snow treads and all will be well. The bus has army personnel on board alongside farming families, and we set off with bright sunlight on fresh snow, and the Armenian church spire on Akdamar Island against the azure sky. A mist soon descends as we begin to climb, and we feel the first ominous slide of tyres on ice. The driver doggedly continues. As we turn a steep bend the bus slides into a steep ditch at the edge of the road and nearly turns over. We are at a precarious angle, and the driver radios for help.

It is minus 10°C outside, so the only option is to stay on board. Snow is falling as the snowplough arrives, and a steel chain is hooked to our bus.

'That chain will break!' I say to the disciple, 'and if the

bus is lifted out, and the chain breaks, it will careen down the mountain!'

We agree to get out of the bus for safety, to the horror of our bus driver, who expects everyone to stay on board. Huddled together in a snow blizzard, we watch the operation and, yes, the chain does break, but fortunately the bus is still lodged in the ditch. We get back on to the bus and within an hour army jeeps and trucks arrive to rescue us. We pile into a jeep and are driven to an army camp nearby, where soldiers serve us bread rolls and delicious thick soup from a huge samovar. We are all cared for with clumsy male gentleness.

The boys sit on the sturdy shoulders of two soldiers, and farming passengers open their bags of goodies, offering salami and dried fruits to everyone. As the bus cannot be retrieved in the snowstorm, we are later ferried back to Van in army trucks, and surprise everyone at the hostel with our unexpected return.

We opt for train travel to Diyarbakir, as the rail line is now cleared of snow, and at 6 am next morning, we slide along footpaths to the station and clamber aboard. It is an old and rather decrepit train, but acceptable after too many near misses on icy roads. It is now clear, a perfect day, and we sit back in our little compartment, delighted with the space to move. We stretch along our seats as the train winds around the lake heading for Diyarbakir. The carriages are like matchboxes, with no heating, and the loo in the final carriage is simply a hole in the floor; we can see the railway track snaking beneath. The idea is to hold onto the railings each side and hope to heaven your aim will find the hole in the floor. BYO loo paper needs to be gripped between your teeth, a highly acrobatic exercise on the swaying train.

Our time in the ancient and walled city of Diyarbakir is marked by Kurdish street protests and angry confrontations with authorities. Kurds are expressing their frustration and helplessness. We see the tents and huts of a huge refugee camp nearby. The Turks are trying to maintain order, and there are claims of human rights abuses emerging. Diyarbakir feels insecure, like a tinderbox about to ignite, so we decide to move on. We take with us indelible memories of Kurdish generosity and friendship, with hopes that one day a sovereign state of Kurdistan may emerge from this region.

Postscript

Partial autonomy for Kurds began in Iraqi Kurdistan in 1991, and this edict has been gathering traction across the region since that time.

Mountains of the Moon, Uganda

*'Over the Mountains of the Moon, ride boldly ride,
if you seek for Eldorado'*

EDGAR ALLAN POE

It is 2006 and we decide to follow our backpacking son's advice to experience the joys of Uganda before the rest of the world arrives. Tourism in this country has been quiet. There are vivid memories of a country battered by tyranny and fear until the removal of Dictator Idi Amin in 1986. A slow recovery has returned a more peaceful way of life and a positive future for this sublimely beautiful country.

Winston Churchill called this former British colony 'The Pearl of Africa', which may have referred to the riches delivered to Britain, rather than its equatorial forests with the world's last large colonies of chimpanzees and gorillas, Africa's highest mountain range, including the fabled Mountains of the Moon, pristine crater lakes and more bird species than anywhere else on earth.

We fly to Entebbe, the former capital, set on the shores of Lake Victoria. There are storks striding the grass beside the runway oblivious to the jet's reverse thrust, and a gentle reminder that we are intruding on their territory. We are shocked by the heat and humidity as we disembark and join a queue that burgeons out from the terminal. Airport staff move slowly and only one immigration post is manned. A three-hour wait for visas is the prospect for most foreigners, with multiple

form filling and verbal interrogation. I silently thank our son for advising us to get our visas in Australia, and we briskly walk through immigration.

We have chosen the Imperial Botanical Hotel adjoining Entebbe's Botanical Gardens on Lake Victoria. Standard hibiscus trees line the driveway with cascading bougainvillea and frangipani trees. There is the heavenly scent of gardenias in the air, made more pungent after the early morning rain. Fish eagles, storks and hornbills perch in the trees, or parade across groomed lawns that slope towards the shore of Lake Victoria. The monkeys jumping and playing in family groups are as much at home here in the hotel grounds as the adjoining Botanical Gardens.

The hotel is grand, indeed 'imperial'. A panel boasts that Bill Clinton stayed here. A Bill Clinton Pavilion was built in his honour, now a popular venue for Ugandan brides. Suddenly there is a roar of police motorbikes leading a six-car procession. We hear it's for a politician's daughter's wedding and watch entranced as the wedding party assembles before proceeding to Bill's Pavilion for a raucous and joyous wedding reception. The bride is a flounce of tulle and lace and six bridesmaids are resplendent in purple-satin sequinned dresses and wreaths of white blossoms, spectacular and exotic against their ebony skin and glossy hair.

We are introduced to Uganda's staple drink, passionfruit juice minus the pips. It is delicious and has reviving qualities to counter the humidity. It is October and the rain usually falls at night, often with dramatic thunder and lightning. The days are balmy and warm. The afternoon is spent swimming in the pool, and watching the fish eagles swoop to the lake to

scoop fish up with their talons, all the while calling out to each other, a running commentary on the success or failure of their venture. A stork lands clumsily on the tree above us and, as darkness falls, crickets and frogs strike up a chorus.

Our plan is to hire a driver and a four-wheel drive for a five-day safari to Murchison Falls, then head west to Fort Portal, and the legendary Ndali Lodge overlooking the Mountains of the Moon (Rwenzori Mountains). We track down a vehicle and a driver, Henry, who speaks English well and is also fluent in five Ugandan languages. Henry is waiting for us at the arranged time of 8 am, immaculate in jeans bomber jacket and trendy reflector sunglasses. He drives with confidence, a great relief to me as it may stop the disciple from back-seat driving during the six-hours to Murchison Falls.

We are surprised to find less traffic and some order to the driving in Uganda, unlike other African countries where it can be not only a nightmare, but a very easy way to end it all. We begin to relax and enjoy the spectacular vegetation as we drive through a tunnel of flowering tree creepers, monkeys and baboons clustered at the roadside, children waving to us in the villages, and undulating hills revealing more hills and forests in the distance. There is a rare ground hornbill strutting across the road, and multi-coloured butterflies catch the brilliant sunlight as they rest on creepers hanging from the tree canopy.

Henry suggests Masindi as our halfway stop. A railroad centre flourished there in the colonial days, and the wonderful Masindi Hotel built in 1920 has generous verandahs draped in vivid bougainvillea. There is a *White Mischief* atmosphere – I can imagine floating chiffons, gin and tonics, the Charleston, and a high time had by all. The hotel has been renovated and

has a good restaurant, and we order spicy curries and stick loyally to the passionfruit juice.

Finally we arrive in Murchison Falls National Park, in the 1960s one of the great tourist meccas with plentiful wildlife and around 12,000 elephants. During the brutal regimes of the 1970s and 1980s, most of the wildlife was destroyed. Since 1986, when stability returned to Uganda, the wildlife numbers have recovered, and tourists are slowly returning.

The park ranger opens the gate and we wind through the lush forest to Sambiya River Lodge, our African-style thatched cottage accommodation. The large restaurant complex, also thatched, is open to the bushland. The cottage features solar-heated water, sensible in Uganda with its frequent power cuts. Waterbuck graze nearby and there are buffalo in the riverbed. A martial eagle flies to its nest clutching a dead mongoose, and the air is filled with the sounds of life in the wild.

There is an eclectic mix of guests, including an 80-year-old American, a former pilot who compares his day's adventures with wartime flying, and calls me 'his little lady' to the amusement of the disciple. He is mesmerised by a group of serious bird-watchers from Belgium. They are in uniform, with matching khaki shorts, vests and floppy hats. There is a delightful group of Dutch hikers, just arrived from Kampala, and in no time, with the aid of many anti-malarial gin and tonics, there is a huge party, which continues through the dinner of delicious curries and fresh tropical fruits.

Guards escort us back to our cottage, as we are after all in the wilds of Uganda, and hyena and elephant sometimes wander through the grounds. We secure the mozzie net and watch the moon cast shadows, the rustles and night calls of bush

life stirring our imagination. Suddenly we wake to a clattering, thudding and grunting; a buffalo herd is moving through the camp. The animals are right outside our window and look fearsome in the moonlight. Sleep returns eventually.

We plan a three-hour boat trip along the Nile to Murchison Falls. Although Victoria Falls bordering Zimbabwe and Zambia is the largest in Africa, Murchison is unusual because the full volume of the Nile cascades through a six-metre aperture. The boat trip is exceptional, revealing an abundance of wildlife along the river. Scores of Nile crocodiles sun themselves along the bank, their jaws wide exposing their dental magnificence, hippos are bathing and elephants saunter through the bushland. The captain wedges the boat between two rocks, near the roaring fall of water, before we gently cruise back to camp.

The drive to Fort Portal takes all day. Finally we climb the road to the crater lake and find Ndali Lodge perched on a narrow ridge overlooking the stark peaks of the Mountains of the Moon. George, an old Ugandan, stokes the lodge's large brick brazier until the coals shimmer, and the pipes from the brazier take hot water to the thatched cottages. Our cottage has a four-poster bed draped with mosquito nets, and chintz cushions cover rattan armchairs on a little terrace overlooking the lake and the distant mountains. As there is no power, dinner is by candlelight, and lanterns light our way back to the cottage. The Mountains of the Moon are now bathed in silver light, and by sheer luck we have a full moon to emphasise their mystical beauty.

Sitting with Bedouin women at the handcrafts market in the Oman Desert, 2003.

The disciple near Khasab, Oman, 2004.

Treating an anaesthetised lion in a ute, Edeni Game Reserve, South Africa, 2005.

Young male elephants checking us out, Kruger National Park, 2006.

With an orphaned cheetah, reared by rangers in South Africa, 2005.

The road to Maree on the Australian Outback Cattle Drive, 2010.

Taking flight to capture rhino with the South African National Parks rhino team, 2009.

Posing with Catherine Hamlin and Geoff Brooks, wildlife photographer, at Monarto Zoo, 2008.

Tilda as Lucia celebrating a Swedish Christmas, 2010.

Soweto by tuk tuk, 2012.

Soweto Theatre Complex, costing $18 million, was completed in 2012.

Refugee camp near Goda in the Ogaden Region, Ethiopia, 1994.

Catherine Hamlin with her golden retriever and patients, the Fistula Hospital, Addis Ababa, 1997.

Catherine, Heather and Sister Marmite at the outpatients village, Desta Mender, Addis Ababa.

Meeting a delegate at the African Women's Conference, Asmara, Eritrea, 1997.

Above: Coffee is brewed at a village inn in northern Ethiopia, 2000.

Left: Mule trek to a monastery, Lalibela, Ethiopia, 2000.

Below: Child shepherds on the road to Axum, 1997.

Africa in the Mallee at Monarto Zoo

'We exist to save animals from extinction'
ROYAL ZOOLOGICAL SOCIETY OF SOUTH AUSTRALIA

A lion roars and a second competes, followed by a duet of growls. Giraffe saunter to the waterhole, where feisty zebra are bucking and kicking at the muddy edge. Waterbuck drink and eland graze quietly nearby. This is not Africa, but Monarto Zoo, 20 kilometres from Murray Bridge and a 40-minute drive from Adelaide.

From the Monarto gatehouse, a four-kilometre road winds through mallee scrubland, part of the 500-hectare free-range area of the park. Here emus and their chicks strut beside the road, kangaroos and wallabies watch the vehicles pass and, on occasion, sleepy lizards hold up visitors as they slowly cross the road.

Animals have right of way at Monarto, the largest open-range zoo in Australia, spreading across 1000 hectares of mallee country. This combination of zoo and natural wilderness sanctuary is, like Adelaide Zoo, under the umbrella of the Royal Zoological Society of South Australia, a not-for-profit organisation that plays a vital role in breeding programs for endangered species, exotic and indigenous.

At the visitor centre, staff direct arrivals towards the

90-minute safari bus tour. The air-conditioned vehicles, with large windows for optimal viewing, cruise through the habitats of cheetah, lion, giraffe, zebra, black and white rhino, hyena, painted dogs, deer and antelope. As the enclosures are so large, it is possible to observe natural animal behaviours, like protection of territory, hierarchical contests between young males of all species, courtship, mating and even births.

Monarto has a herd of 34 giraffe, and five births have been viewed from safari buses by visitors. A giraffe gives birth standing up. Within an hour the dropped calf will be on its feet, ready to move to safety with its mother, as in the wild the afterbirth smell attracts predators.

These insights into animal behaviour are provided on the bus by Monarto's team of 85 volunteer tour guides. Dressed bush style, and full of passion and dedication (often combined with ribald humour), these volunteers are outstanding ambassadors for Monarto and for the conservation of wildlife in general.

The southern white rhino exhibit is significant. There have been two recent births at Monarto. This gravely endangered gentle giant can weigh 2500 kilograms and, despite a ferocious reputation in the wild, Monarto's six residents are used to human contact and are gentle and curious around people. They like to wallow in mud baths during the heat of the day, and the two-month-old baby is delighting visitors with his joy of mud slides. After squelching and rolling in the mud, he looks like a fat chocolate baby.

White rhino numbers in Africa were down to just 100 in 1900 and, although there are successful breeding programs and the worldwide population is now around 7000, they are still greatly at risk. Poachers kill them and saw off their horns, which are ground into powder and used for medicinal remedies and aphrodisiacs in some Asian cultures.

Monarto is pioneering novel ways of educating and hopefully, inspiring people about animals and their conservation by providing opportunities for closer contact. There are safari bus stops at the rhino bomas, and the African waterhole habitat, with walking trails linking the cheetah enclosure to the giraffe platform. Keepers will introduce a rhino to visitors, allowing for closer contact, and after patting a rhino you can believe the old saying about the thick skin. But I can attest that tickling a rhino under the thigh is like touching pure silk.

A 500-metre walking track connects the rhino boma to the cheetah platform. This botanical walk passes flourishing young native callitris pines, the endangered Monarto mint bush and dagger-leafed wattles established by the zoo's team of land-care volunteers. Known as the Mallee Minders, they spend Wednesdays working in the scrub, their red painted truck known as the red devil is often loaded with crates of tube stock to be planted, and concoctions to destroy the feral plants introduced by our early settlers.

About 500 hectares of Monarto is open mallee woodland, and after 14 years of care is becoming a pristine example of mallee country. Echidna diggings can be seen, and with luck it is possible to see this waddling animal, one of this planet's oldest surviving mammals, its closest relative the platypus. Echidnas are timid and will dig rapidly in rotary fashion if they are detected. A research team at Monarto is monitoring echidna movements, foraging patterns and home range by following known individuals, distinguished by coloured tags.

The cheetah platform is approached by a walkway elevated

to allow for excellent viewing of the habitat below. Cheetah are greatly endangered in southern Africa, and now extinct in northern Africa and Asia. Monarto's two recent litters are the first cheetah to be born in Australia for 13 years; one litter of six cubs, their mother unable to feed them, was hand-reared by Monarto's keepers. This has helped the Meet the Cheetah program flourish. As you pat and stroke the cheetah you may hear a purr that sounds like an idling car engine.

Beyond the cheetah habitat is 60 hectares of grassland. Plans are afoot to develop a Serengeti exhibit of African animals, conduct game drives and walks, and construct safari-styled accommodation for overnight stays.

From the cheetah platform a walking track winds through the mallee trees and callitris pines to the Waterhole bus stop, and the giraffe platform. Monarto's 34 giraffe, including very young calves, can be viewed from here, or the elevated walkway. Their huge eyes are rimmed by long curly eyelashes, and children watch in awe as a 45-centimetre tongue curls around a willow branch and the giraffe draw the leaves into its mouth.

From the giraffe platform, eland, waterbuck and zebra can also be observed, and the large waterhole means there are many varieties of birds, including stilts and plovers. This is also a perfect vantage point to watch animal interactions. A volunteer guide is stationed at the platform to answer questions.

The lion enclosure was opened by the Honourable Michael Rann, Premier of South Australia in 2003, and to the delight of the busload of media representatives, his silver car was chased by a lion. Monarto's pride has now been boosted by the arrival of two male cubs. Their antics, once they emerged from their cubbing den into the main habitat, enthrall crowds. A Meet the

Lions program is available to visitors for a closer introduction to the beasts and a chance to learn more from their keepers.

With the success of these programs, a Working with Wildlife tour was established allowing visitors to work with animal management staff for a day, and gain an entertaining insight into life behind the scenes at the Zoo. Visitors can help care for endangered Australian species, such as the Tasmanian devil, see a lion tooth filled at the surgery, observe a birth or the fostering of orphaned joeys by female wallabies, prepare food for meerkats or feed the bilbies.

Zoos need, and can be catalysts for conservation, loudly beating a warning drum. Each time a tree is lopped in what is left of the wild, animals are threatened and the ecological balance damaged. We need to restore this balance between animals, habitats and human life; remember extinction is forever.

The Hidden Delights of a Smuggler's Port

'Time and tide makes us mercenaries all'
PATRICK ROTHFUSS

The runway at Seeb Airport in Muscat shimmers with mirages. The desert is interrupted by mountains to the west and the turquoise Gulf of Oman to the east. A small propjet will take us to Khasab at the entrance to the Persian Gulf on the Musandam Peninsula, where rocky mountains form spectacular fjords and coral reefs provide diving grounds. We look insipidly Western beside the other passengers in traditional Omani dress, Indians wearing turbans, and Arab men in dishdasha accompanied by their veiled wives.

We fly low over Musandam, and down a narrow mountain pass to land at Khasab. It is late in the afternoon and the mountains are golden pink. There are no taxis, so we sit on our cases waiting for the promised transfer. Our Croatian pilot walks past and obligingly uses his mobile phone to remind the hotel of our arrival, and ten minutes later Mohammed arrives, white robed and turbaned. He had been watching the cricket and apologises profusely.

We want to visit the port and he has to return to the hotel so without hesitation he hands us the keys to his car. Off we go, on the right side of the road, trying to avoid herds of goats and wandering pedestrians, as well as other cars, with drivers, unlike us, who appear to know where they are going. We are hoping to see the Iranian smugglers leave for Bander Abbas, an Iranian port on the other side of the Persian Gulf. Eighty or so boats arrive in Khasab every morning from about 6 am after a two-hour speedboat ride. The speedboat engines have been super-charged to outrun the Iranian coast guard. The smugglers wear their turbans with attitude; reflector sunglasses and mobile phones complete the look. Their day is spent in Khasab at the souk buying goods unavailable at home, mainly American cigarettes. There is much socialising and tea drinking to seal the deals, and at 6 pm they noisily depart for Bander Abbas with their contraband.

We arrive at the port early. The speedboats are lined up amid great activity of loading, stacking and securing the bounty. An Arabian fishing dhow has just moored and brightly veiled women are bargaining with the fishermen. The deck of the dhow sparkles with kingfish, and sea birds swoop and caw; beyond the breakwater another fishing dhow is approaching. The first Iranian smuggler is ready to go, and he gives a thumbs-up to his mate. He then dramatically revs the engine and takes off at great speed.

We decide Mohammed might be concerned about his car, so we reluctantly leave to find our hotel. This proves to be a problem as Khasab, an ancient trading port, has winding streets with frequent goat hazards and small market squares. After some marital disharmony, my husband and I agree on a direction and by sheer luck find the hotel. We arrive as the call to prayer echoes from the little mosque nearby and a mist hangs over the

pink mountains promising a vivid sunset. Mohammed wants to discuss cricket, not smugglers, and as alcohol is not available, we have a sundowner of mango juice on ice and watch the last red streaks of sunset fade into the desert night.

Ships' Buoys in Valletta

'Discoveries are often made ... by going off the main road'

FRANK TYGER

After months of grey skies and drizzle, I have a primeval urge that is becoming an obsession, to zip open the sky in order to glimpse blueness and light. As a respite from gloomy London, Georgie and I decide the cheapest and fastest sunlight escape is to Malta. We have a two-week break from our work at Australia House, so we secure a holiday package to Malta using a hole-in-the-wall travel agent in Piccadilly Circus.

Traffic problems to Heathrow have me boarding as the gates close. Georgie is relieved to see me, but the economy section has been overbooked and there are no spare seats. A British Airways hostess ushers us to the front of the plane where two plush leather seats in first class are offered. For the next few hours we enjoy a delightful flight of champagne and heady indulgence, manna from heaven to Aussie sheilas on a working holiday.

Soon the pilot circles over what looks like an island of golden sandcastles. It is Valletta, basking in late afternoon sunlight, the sunbaked fortress around the harbour contrasting with the deep blue of the Mediterranean Sea. The Maltese islands are a group of barren rocks jutting out of the ocean, and for centuries have been at the crossroads of trading routes and warring empires. There are no rivers, and the highest cliff top registers 300 metres above sea level. The islands were first settled by Sicilians in 4000 BC; Phoenicians later named them Malta, meaning refuge. The wars versus refuge history has included occupation by Arabs, Normans and the Hapsburgs.

Valletta was built in 1500 AD as a fortified stronghold, and became a flourishing centre for trade and learning with a university, palaces and ornate churches. Napoleon claimed Malta in 1798 and in 1800 it was the turn of the British to take control, finally relinquishing to the Maltese in 1947.

Our travel package has us staying in a small private hotel in Sliema, not far from Valletta, with the promise of a nearby beach. At breakfast we notice this beach is a stretch of rocks with slivers of sand and, although not promising, the blue sky and sun is mesmerising and affirms our desire to become sun-worshipping Druids for two weeks.

We notice a well-dressed solitary male taking breakfast at a corner table. He constantly glances our way, sighing and returning to his Italian papers. He has dark hair, curling at the temples and an interesting profile complete with Roman nose – which my mother would describe as aristocratic. He checks his watch and folds his paper, slotting it into his briefcase, and approaches us with a bow of introduction. He takes Georgie's hand and plants a gentle kiss, and then it is my turn. Marco is the new Italian Consul to Malta. He moans about his new posting in heavily accented English, saying he is now living with barbarians and his Valletta residence is not ready so he has been parked here in Sliema with a Fiat 500 while his Alfa Romeo Spider remains in Rome. How will he put up with this new life after Paris, and would we join him for dinner to relieve a mortifying life he has been assigned to for the next

three years? His eyes are twinkling with amusement as he sees us sympathise with his predicament and accept his offer.

'Maybe his wife is still in Rome with the Alfa Spider?' I say to Georgie, but we are happy to have found a host and protector and over the next two days we squeeze into his Fiat 500 and head off to see the Malta hidden away from the tourist enclaves along the coastline.

Marco makes a five-minute stop at the Consulate each day to clear his diary of meetings with barbarians, and we then drive away, the little engine roaring in protest. He drives as if he is at the wheel of his Alfa, with Latin bravado to impress us. We have the windows down and the sunroof open to allow fresh air to temper the heat of the day, not to mention Marco's Sobranie cigarette smoke.

Today we are heading for Lija, a small village in the centre of Malta surrounded by bountiful citrus orchards. The village motto is *'Suavi Fructu Rubeo' (With Tasty Fruit I Blossom)*. An avenue of flowering oleander trees leads to the central plaza and a baroque parish church boasting Guiseppe Cali frescoes winding around its ceilings. Marco lifts his lead foot from the accelerator as we take narrow one-way lanes under the carved stone archways. Wealthy Maltese families chose to live in Lija, away from the bustle of Valletta. They built Sicilian-inspired mansions with exquisite courtyard gardens and tinkling fountains with water playing over Rubenesque statues. Gardens are shaded by trees pregnant with luscious fruit, and exotic flowers carpet the walls and garden beds.

We park the little Fiat and wander, noticing that Marco's scathing opinion of living with barbarians is softening amid such elegance and historic style. Lija is stirring as locals emerge

from siesta to sit around doorways under balconies dripping with red geraniums. Families and neighbours chat together as their children play in the street. Marco walks between us with a swagger and grins at the jibes from locals assessing the two blondes at his side. He calmly draws on his Sobranie and a smoke ring wafts into the air as he shepherds us along the laneways. He is stylish in a crumpled cream linen suit; Georgie and I are clichés of London's Kings Road, the cutting-edge shopping street in swinging sixties London, with our bright mini skirts, frilled sun tops, strappy sandals and outsized sunglasses – Georgie's in pink and mine circular and framed in white. Mary Quant would be proud of us.

There is excitement in the streets. Tonight's fireworks display will bring thousands of people to Lija for the Christian festa, celebrated each August. It is late in the afternoon and there is a carnival atmosphere as pop-up food kiosks appear selling homemade marmalades, classic Maltese treacle and candied orange rings, orange blossom honey and locally pressed olive oil. Stalls sell table linen of traditional bobbin lace stitched *guipure* style and featuring the eight-pointed Maltese cross.

We stop at a little restaurant famous for rustic Maltese food and order *aljotta*, the traditional seafood soup, with freshly warmed pita bread. A Sicilian desert of sponge cake mixed with ice cream follows, and reviving pomegranate tea. We are transfixed as Marco talks of Mediterranean maritime history, his passion and specialty at university; he seems to be enjoying the rapt attention from his naive audience.

We notice the crowds are milling towards the main square where the festa procession is to begin, and life-sized statues of Christ and the saints are paraded. Most local villagers take part,

and after speeches from religious dignitaries the skies light up with a fireworks display confirming Maltese pyrotechnics as second to none. Lija erupts with noise and the technicolour sparkles and flashes from above seem to ignite the music and dancing on the streets, which will no doubt continue until dawn.

As Marco has an early morning flight to Rome, we reluctantly cram into the little Fiat and speed off to Sliema taking with us indelible memories of Lija. There are hugs and kisses of farewell and we realise we shall miss our genial and enigmatic host, despite his foul Russian cigarettes and terrifying driving. All his moaning and sighing masks a noble soul who has been delightful company.

Determined to go back to London suntanned, we decide to spend a day at the beach. Wearing bikinis and a thick coating of coconut oil we wander down to the seashore. My flowerpot hat is scattered with daisies and Georgie's has a large sunflower emblazoned on the brim. We are the only sunbathers there, and soon realise this is a local beach for fishermen, with boats and dinghies laden with nets and fish containers. Nets are being untangled and holes mended, as the latest fish harvest is loaded onto trailers for market. It is not long before we notice a steady stream of uninvited guests sitting around us on the rocks. They are quite harmless and friendly but we feel vulnerable while on show.

I have a brainwave. A fisherman by the water's edge has a dinghy near his fishing ketch, and I ask him if we could hire it for the afternoon. We agree on a price and soon Georgie and I are rowing out to the centre of Valletta Harbour to a large buoy. We tether the dinghy to the buoy, spread our towels along the planked seats and apply more coconut oil. We blissfully sunbake

in peace, gently floating on the glassy water. Georgie's transistor is tuned to Radio Caroline, the British pirate radio station that broadcasts from the English Channel, and, for a moment, all is well with the world. Suddenly we hear shouts and laughter and see a 15-metre sloop under sail approaching us, with a guy on the bow yelling, 'I'll bet they're Aussies!'

'Of course we are, and have you any Vegemite?' we reply, and accept their offer for a tow back to shore. I catch the rope and tie a knot to the metal ring on the dinghy whilst Georgie uncouples the oars and places them in the hull. Sails are lowered and the engine gurgles into action, then with a swish we are skimming behind the yacht's wake at high speed.

The yacht *Penida* was built in Penang by Roderick, who is at the helm. He is a 50-ish American, short and stocky with hair greying at the temples and green eyes. 'Pen' is for Penang, and '-ida' represents Florida, his destination. Rod has picked up and dropped off crews over the past months sailing from Penang to India, the Middle East and Suez Canal. Sue and Andy with four-year-old Max and two-year-old Johnno boarded in Greece. Andy and Sue are Australians, based in London with years of sailing experience and a love of ocean-racing yachts, and they will spend a month as crew before Andy returns to work in London. Freddie from Plymouth boarded in Suez, having worked on cruise ships in the Mediterranean. He's accepted a free passage home in return for crew duties. He looks like a hippy with his long tangled locks and flowered board shorts.

We return our dinghy to the fisherman, who has been watching our tow-in with a group of his mates. They seem suitably impressed by our glamorous arrival, and help us ashore

and bid us farewell like old friends. We watch *Penida* head off for the marina amid hearty waves and yells of 'see you later' from all aboard.

It is sunset when we arrive at the marina and board the yacht for the first time. Our new friends have two days to stretch their legs on terra firma, see the sights of Malta and stock up on supplies for the next leg of their voyage. We meet each day for meals or sightseeing and then, out of the blue, Rod suggests we join them for the voyage to Sicily, we can help Sue with the boys and be part of the crew; perhaps we could fly back to London from Palermo? So we change flights and cancel accommodation in an afternoon of flurry and early next morning walk our luggage to the marina to set sail.

The main cabin on *Pernida* has a galley with four bunks, the bow has two narrow bunk beds and a hatch for our luggage, with a tiny porthole.

'A bit like sleeping in a sardine can,' I say to Georgie.

There is a cupboard-sized loo and washbasin for all of us adjacent to our digs. This is a real sailing yacht and conditions are spartan but adequate. I am interested to see how safe Max and Johnno will be when we set sail. Sue tells me they wear harnesses clipped to the railings when they are on deck, and below deck they are free to move about and play.

A brisk wind means we can depart under sail, and we soon realise the need for silence and obedience as orders are shouted – or more specifically sworn – and sails are hoisted. The booms from the mainsails are a lethal weapon if you lose concentration when we are changing tack. It is exhilarating to see the sails fill and our speed increase as the wind takes hold of the canvas and tips us to a 40-degree angle, splicing the swell ahead.

The Valletta fortress diminishes into the horizon as we head due north for Sicily. We are now in open sea and hear only flapping sails and the swish of water against the hull as we dip and curve through the ocean. A pod of dolphins discover us and play at the bow, jumping and dancing together, disappearing and then minutes later returning for an even more flamboyant performance. Sea birds caw and, like silver flashes of light emerging from the depths, there are flying fish to the side of us, reflecting the sun in their gauzy fins, like fairy wings. There is a timelessness, a feeling of being part of nature's plan, where we can contemplate the secrets of marine life – maybe life itself.

Later we help Sue in the galley and prepare a hearty stew, served with pita bread, with fruit to follow and strong sweet tea. Stories are read to Max and Johnno, who are tucked up head to toe in a cot with high sides that can be strapped securely in rough weather.

Night falls and we decide to stay on deck, with the Milky Way lighting the sky and moonlight playing with the phosphorescence of breaking waves. Andy, Rod and Freddie take three-hour shifts at the helm throughout the night. We learn how to calculate our position using a sextant, and take turns at the wheel, trying to obey strong commands and ignore the expletives when we turn the wrong way. Freddie seems to know every constellation in the northern sky. It is strange for us to look up and not find the Southern Cross.

This pattern of life at sea continues. We mend sails by darning the holes or splits with strong twine; we fish, cook, babysit and can choose to chat or spend time in complete solitude. My favourite place is the bow railing with legs akimbo just watching the sea.

    The wind drops and we are becalmed, so it is safe to swim. Rod produces cakes of soap that lather in seawater, so we all jump overboard for a much needed hair wash and body scrub. We then clamber back on board to await the wind, which begins later in the day. We are slowly approaching Sicily's southern coast. It is nightfall and we weigh anchor in a little cove with a few lights sprinkled around its curve. It is far too hot to sleep below deck, so we take our mattresses aloft and spread out, totally exhausted. The men are relieved they are no longer on night duty, and soon the air resonates with their robust snores.

    We are woken at dawn by excited cries and chatter around our yacht. Dinghy loads of villagers have come to inspect the anchored intruder and its occupants. We speak smatterings of Italian, and agree to come ashore with them, eat their seafood and explore the village, the locals as happy to accept our cash as we are to be on dry land and accept their hospitality.

    We have a farewell dinner by campfire on the beach, with half the village taking part. The accordions are playing, there is dancing, local wine, cheeses and pastas, with the Sicilian mammas firmly directing proceedings.

    The following morning, Georgie and I catch a local bus to Palermo, taking memories that will remain with us forever.

Catherine Hamlin and the Fistula Hospital, Ethiopia (1994)

'What we have done for ourselves alone, dies with us; what we have done for others remains immortal'

ALFRED PIKE

It is 1994 and I am in Ethiopia with a small international delegation from UNICEF. We are to report on how aid money has been spent following the devastating years of famine that prompted a global monetary response. Since the famine, Mengistu's terror regime in Addis Ababa has been overthrown. Tigreans from the north of Ethiopia are now in power, and a tentative peace between the warring tribes seems to reign in this battered and destitute country.

I have read about an extraordinary Australian doctor working in Addis and, during our final days in Ethiopia, organise time out from UNICEF duties to visit her. Addis is overrun with homeless people, many are wounded soldiers, some are young women with babies and toddlers clinging to their skirts. The central median strip through the city is crammed with makeshift shelters, where people sleep under trees and huddle together in small groups.

We are driving to the river that winds through Addis, my driver trying to dodge enormous potholes as well as donkeys laden with goods, and the odd herd of goats shepherded by

barefooted youths using long sticks to smack them into line. The air is pristine and crisp, more to do with the altitude being 2500 metres above sea level than a clear and clean environment. Rubbish litters the pavements and a recent rain shower has added a mudslide for locals to navigate as they head to Addis Mercato, Africa's largest market place.

Despite confronting and extreme poverty, there are wonderful sights of young girls with braided hair and brightly coloured clothes laughing together, children with high cheek bones and bushy hair playing in muddy alleyways, their white teeth flashing against glossy black skin. They are show-stoppingly beautiful.

Market stalls line the streets with oranges, mandarins and bananas, but not much else. The shoemakers fashion thongs and sandals out of old car tyres; floor rugs are made from brightly coloured woven rags. Such ingenuity of re-cycling can be seen in every street of the Mercato. Women, bent double, are carrying mounds of firewood on their backs for cooking fires and to warm their huts against the extreme cold of night.

To my amazement, we are soon driving through a lush forest of blue gums, the air pungent with the smell of eucalyptus. The driver tells me that Emperor Menelik, who ruled Ethiopia in the early 1900s, planted Australian blue gums in the circle of hills that surround Addis Ababa. With the black volcanic soil and ample rainfall, they have thrived. We finally stop at a large iron gate, with the sign Addis Ababa Fistula Hospital, and notice a queue of local people clustered in small groups patiently waiting to enter.

Catherine walks briskly towards me. She is very tall, reed slim and wears a white lab coat; a stethoscope dangles around

her neck. Her blue eyes smile as she welcomes me with a hug. She has just finished morning surgery. 'Let's go to the cottage for tea and a chat about Adelaide,' she says.

Catherine and her husband Reg worked as obstetrician/gynaecologists at the Queen Victoria Hospital in Adelaide, before moving to Ethiopia in 1958. Here they established a hospital to focus on fistula surgery for women suffering from obstructed labour in childbirth. Since then, tens of thousands of young women have been saved from appalling outcomes by the Hamlins. In most cases, fistula surgery is a relatively simple procedure, allowing the women to return to their villages completely cured. Ethiopia has hundreds of remote rural villages in rugged and impregnable terrain, with no medical aid close by. Obstructed labour may continue for ten days before a stillborn baby is born and the mother suffers a fistula split between her vagina and bladder or bowel. Incontinence and the unpleasant smell causes rejection by her husband and other villagers and eventual isolation. The Hamlins recognised this urgent problem in the 1950s and now, 50 years later, the centre they established is the best facility in the world addressing obstetric fistula problems.

We walk down steep steps through beautiful gardens to a whitewashed cottage, with climbing roses and wisteria draped over the verandah. Inside there are chintzy sofas, a piano, a desk piled high with papers, and two boisterous Labradors. They greet us lovingly as a gentle Ethiopian girl tries to set out tea and shortbreads, completely ignoring Catherine's orders to sit.

There were complications during this morning's three-hour operation on a 16-year-old girl.

'She is fine and will make a full recovery,' Catherine says.

'Her father carried her on his back for ten days from the Semien mountains to Addis Ababa, accepting cart rides where possible, but mostly travelling by foot.'

He has been billeted with a local family until his daughter is strong enough to make the long journey home.

We chat together, and I discover Catherine loves wildlife as much as she loves saving human life. Over the years she and her family have safaried and camped in the wilds of Africa, and she is knowledgeable about captive breeding of endangered rhinoceros, part of my work and passion at Monarto Zoo in Adelaide. She looks at her watch and tells me she's expecting the arrival of three Harley Street specialists, and asks if I would like to join her in the wards. We are followed by the dogs, who take up residence under the patients' beds, and are much loved by all at the hospital. As this is not strictly within the protocols of a London hospital, and with the doctors approaching us, Catherine stands tall, and with a wave of her arms loudly commands: 'Shoo dogs! Shoo!!' They get up with tails wagging and bound outside through the open doorway, only to stealthily re-enter by a side door to take up position under the beds again.

The Fistula Hospital has strong support from the UK and Australia, and the three British surgeons are here for one month in an honorary capacity, to perform highly intricate bladder repair for patients who have such severe damage to their organs, they require grafts or transplants. Some girls are badly crippled from months – sometimes even years – of sitting isolated in a hut, dripping with urine and faecal matter. They need to learn to walk again, and a wing of the hospital is devoted to physiotherapy and remedial exercise programs to help them regain muscle strength and mobility.

This morning spent with Catherine registers ten on my Richter scale of wake-up calls, and from this short visit there germinates a strong friendship that has spanned two decades, with frequent visits to Catherine and the hospital looped into my Rhino conservation trips to southern Africa. Catherine stories are legion. Those of her strength, humility, Christian values and care of Ethiopian women are well known, but I have been privileged to get to know her sense of the ridiculous, dry humour, love of fun and gossip and passion for gardens.

On one visit, we were being driven by Catherine to church and were running late for the service. My husband was in the front seat clutching the window strap and stifling gasps as Catherine sped through Addis traffic, swerving past mini buses, dodging donkeys and goat herds, bumping over potholes, and then wheeling round the roundabouts with speed-ace style. He suggested he'd rather walk home after church, to which she replied, 'Alfie, you'd get lost, you'd better stick with me!' The church service was a combination of Anglican tradition with African exuberance, and the church resonated with chants, robust singing and clapping. The congregation looked exotic in Ethiopian dress, making us feel drab and boring in our beige linens.

Ethiopia is predominantly Christian Orthodox, tracing its beginnings to the glorious legends of Sheba, Queen of Ethiopia, and King Solomon. Christianity replaced Ethiopia's worship of the Serpent in the 1st century AD, and since that time the Church has played an integral role in all aspects of Ethiopian life, socially and politically.

In 2004, Oprah Winfrey discovered Catherine's work and invited her to be a special guest on her TV program in America.

This resulted in huge interest and generosity from viewers, plus a hefty personal cheque from Oprah. The money funded a much needed surgical unit, built adjacent to the hospital. In 2005, the private jet was winging its way to Addis Ababa with Oprah onboard. During her visit to Catherine, she met patients and delighted staff by wearing traditional Ethiopian dress for photographs, and lighting up the hospital with her generous personality and vigour.

Catherine makes regular visits to Australia, to visit her family and usually with an itinerary crammed with public speaking appointments and media interviews. In 2008, aged 85, she arrived in Adelaide, and despite a very long international flight we immediately drove 90 kilometres to Monarto Zoo to see the new baby rhino, before returning to Adelaide, where she speaks to a group of medicos at the Women's and Children's Hospital. The next morning, she was up at dawn, ready to take a flight to Sydney for her next round of talks.

In 2009, the realisation of Catherine's dream ('To make sure my work continues long after I'm gone!') is realised with the opening of a midwifery college at Desta Mender, the outpatient village that lies in beautiful farmland on the outskirts of Addis Ababa. The three-year midwifery course trains Ethiopian girls from all over the country to be midwives, linking their villages to primary health care and delegating them with the authority to direct pregnant women to seek early hospital attention if an obstructed labour is diagnosed. By having expertise in prenatal care at village level, the instance of fistulas should eventually cease, the trained village midwives the stepping stones in bringing rural Ethiopia to the modern world of medicine.

The opening is attended by the Ethiopian president and

health and welfare ministers, as well as consular dignitaries from Australia and the United Kingdom. The weather is perfect. Marquees have been set up around the small lake near the entrance to Desta Mender. Grand speeches punctuate the spicy Ethiopian feast, and then ribbons are cut to allow honoured guests to wander around the buildings of the new college. I am proud to see Australia has been a principal donor to this project. In 2012 I attend the first graduation of midwives; 20 girls wearing tasselled mortarboards and accompanied by proud families receive their degrees. Catherine proudly tells me that the student intake is expanding and the degree at the college is now recognised as a benchmark by top medical bodies and hospitals in Ethiopia.

It is now 2014, and Catherine has celebrated her 90th birthday. She is still actively involved at the hospital and the Ethiopian Government nominated her for this year's Nobel Peace Prize.

Refugees in the Ogaden, Ethiopia (1994)

*'Taking my mother's hand, I whispered:
"Are we really safe now?"'*

CHILD REFUGEE

There are 90 young children, in nine rows of ten, sitting on the floor of a small makeshift classroom. We are near the town of Mekelle in Tigray, a northern province of Ethiopia that borders Eritrea. Bright eyes are watching the teacher write in Tigrinya script on a small blackboard. This language is Semitic in origin and closely related to Amharic, so well understood further south. There is not a sound, not even a wriggle as they listen. We are watching the children from behind, amazed at their decorum and discipline. The teacher then beckons us to come forward and she and her class give us a rousing welcome with claps and cheers.

I am on an Ethiopian field trip as part of a UNICEF delegation, visiting areas where UNICEF has worked hard to bring education and medical care to children after years of famine and war. Our brief is to report on how aid money has been spent, and to relay this information to our respective countries and UNICEF members back home.

The Tigray now hold power in Ethiopia after overthrowing Mengistu's terror regime in 1991. There is a tentative truce between them and the Amhara, who are ethnically and

culturally a different tribe. The fact that schools are up and running is a plus, but it is obvious that there are no books or pencils, no paper – or any form of teaching aids. These 90 young children will go home at lunchtime, to be replaced by another 90 children for the afternoon session and yes, it is the same teacher who is caring for and trying to teach 180 children each day in this small classroom. (Through UNICEF in Addis we subsequently organise the shipment of teacher aids, pens and exercise books to this school.)

There are seven of us in the delegation representing First World countries, accompanied by Western media, an Ethiopian doctor and government officials. Tonight we are staying on a hill just out of Mekelle in an old fortress hotel boasting turrets and a moat-like ramp; there are no moats or water. Water is like gold in this part of Tigray. We find a bucket of water in each room, and although the hotel has no power, we attend an extraordinary dinner in the banquet hall, where goat meat has been cooked over coals.

Our hosts, chiefs of the Tigrayan People's Liberation Front, are currently in Mekelle and were informed of our visit. No doubt all eight men have brutal warrior history, but tonight there is no evidence of soldier's kit, and I'm happy the AK47s are out of sight. We sit in a little block together and listen to endless speeches and translations of glorious fighting and victories gained through their bravery, while we spare a thought for landmines and limbless children and famine-starved people. It is pretty hard to grow food and tend herds in the middle of a war zone, and it is also hard to be polite and applaud the diatribe we are listening to, but we do so and UNICEF is welcomed and thanked. We doubt if they have any real appreciation of the work that is currently being done by NGOs and donor countries.

A sleepless night is spent fending off mozzies with Rid; there are no mosquito nets. The bedroom is at ground level, so at dawn I break out through the window and elude a sleeping guard at the gate to walk outside the barricades and watch a heaven-sent sunrise of mellow pinks lighting the countryside. I return to ablutions with the bucket of water even including a quick hair wash, and after energy bars and a coffee, our little convoy heads off to nearby woods to inspect an open-air school, mercifully with more teaching aids, but no classroom. When it rains, there's no school.

We then visit recently sunk water wells, guaranteeing clean water that will instantly reduce child mortality. There have been many wells sunk in this area by UNICEF. Nearby there is a recently constructed diesel-powered mill, a life-changing progression from the stone grinding of grain, requiring hours of back-breaking toil by women. All these developments are at grassroots level, but are already having a major impact on the health and wellbeing of the community.

Our time in Tigray is up. We leave early to allow for an estimated three hours of security checks at Mekelle airport. This paranoia is a result of the war; security is so tight, it feels like a current war zone. Soldiers and guards are armed with the dreaded AK47s and they are at the gates, the small terminal and the pathway to the tarmac. Our paperwork is scrutinised and our visas studied with ferocious attention, and then a full-body search is directed and we are segregated into black-curtained booths, one for males and one for females. My female handler is so thorough, it jangles every retaliatory impulse in my body, but instead of kicking her in fury, I start giggling. Suddenly

her face breaks into a glorious smile and we laugh together, the tension instantly defused.

Our Dutch delegate made repeated requests to authorities that a refugee camp in the troubled Ethiopian province of Ogaden be included on our itinerary. Her requests were ignored, but she has been persisting and with mention of a pending discussion back home of future funding options, the visit is reluctantly granted and will be included as part of our field trip.

There are two days of debrief meetings with UNICEF in Addis, before we squeeze into a single-engine UN plane for our flight to Gode, in the Ogaden. Bordering Somalia, and populated by ethnic Somali Moslems, the Ogaden has been a troubled area of Ethiopia for decades. Counter insurgency and ethnic genocide displaced civilian populations and created a tug of war between Christian Orthodox Ethiopia and Moslem Somalia. The refugee camp we are visiting is home to 40,000 displaced civilians from Somalia. Classified as Ethiopia's Somali state, the Ogaden is semi-arid but subject to severe droughts. The current drought is right up there with the worst on record.

Pieter our pilot is a delightful South African. As our group fill the six passenger seats, he offers me the co-pilot seat, and I have a chance to chat with him en route. He was a bush pilot in South Africa, and jumped at the offer to work as a United Nations pilot based in Addis Ababa. He is concerned that we depart Gode by 4 pm as this plane has no instruments and sunset is scheduled to be around 6 pm in Addis tonight, allowing for the two-hour flight. Our little plane swings and sways as the thermals play with us in the clearest of blue skies. After leaving

green and lush Addis, the terrain below broadens to scorched arid and bare desert country. There are hills but no trees.

Pieter lands on a dusty strip and we are met by a team from Médecins Sans Frontières, stationed at the refugee camp. UNICEF has provided a water-treatment plant near the polluted Wabi Shebelle river that passes through Gode on its way to Somalia. Two French doctors will escort us round the camp. We drive over a small rise and see before us a camp of thatched and conical *tukuls* stretching across a three-mile radius, housing 40,000 refugees. There is not one tree in sight, just sameness. These are the forgotten people of the Ogaden that both Ethiopia and Somalia would prefer to ignore, blaming each other for its existence. Lack of good nutrition and clean water have riddled the camp with disease and child mortality. Now, the severe drought has thwarted any possibility of cultivation, coupled with warlord politics, making the fate of these 40,000 people precarious if not hopeless.

The French doctors are over-worked and tired, but their passion and dedication to what they are doing puts them at the coalface of human compassion and care. The punishing hours and lack of facilities is an added pressure, but their tented hospital is spotless, the patients clean and cared for. But loss of life, particularly babies and young children from malnutrition, is constantly confronting and devastating to the medical corps.

We then drive down to the brown slick of pollution that is the river Wabi Shebelle, the water-treatment plant on its banks processing clean drinking water, a major health improvement for the camp. We are invited to visit families in their *tukul* huts and walk along the neat rows, swamped by children of all ages,

laughing playing and skipping around us. We give out pens and notebooks to shrieks of delight and realise that the resilience of children in appalling conditions can't be destroyed if they have food in their tummies, and friends to play with. These children have survived war and village displacement, but most have their families with them.

We are invited into a *tukul*, welcomed by a young couple with their three children. It is now 40°C outside, but inside there is shade and protection with the conical roof providing lofty space. The cross beams networking the ceiling are covered by neatly folded bedding and clothes. A cooking pot and utensils sit in one corner with small stools nearby, and the dirt floor is groomed and swept to perfection. There is pride and order in this *tukul*, seven years their home.

We return to the Médecins Sans Frontières compound to lunch with medical staff and hear about their work lives. They are required to have two weeks away from camp after four weeks work, to preserve sanity and health. These are exceptional people who silently work at the frontline of human desperation, emanating selflessness and a passion to make a difference, and we conclude that they would not choose any other vocation.

We hear about politics in the area, which is a disaster. It is warlord territory, and we are told that the resident warlord has ordered our presence at his quarters at 3 pm. We drive to a walled area and notice precious water leaking through the iron gates manned by a group of teenagers with AK47s pointed at our car. They wear Nike peaked caps and camouflage gear and saunter over to us with brash nonchalance, before opening the gate to allow us through. An intricate sprinkler system is watering ferns and plants in a lush garden; ahead is a mansion, its roof spiked with antennae, satellite dishes and myriad communication aerials. And there are crates of UNICEF-branded pharmaceuticals, sitting outside in the 40°C heat!

We are escorted along a walkway by the armed youths, joined by three more before entering a foyer where we are told to wait. After 40 minutes of feeling corralled by our captors, we ask how long we must wait to meet their leader, as our plane must depart by 4 pm. This message is relayed and the door opens and three older men appear. We follow them to a meeting room and sit facing the leader and his men. The leader wears two Rolex watches, one on each arm and grins sheepishly at us. Through interpreters he is told we are from UNICEF. He asks what UNICEF means, but is interrupted by the deafening sounds of a hovering military helicopter that lands noisily beside the building. He is much more interested in his mercenaries manoeuvres than our presence and we are quickly dismissed.

It is not difficult to work out what is happening here, with fighting happening just 160 kilometres away in Somalia. Our Dutch delegate has had good reason to question funding and the financing of these warlord outposts in the Ogaden. We leave hurriedly in our car, but are followed by the warlord's hoons. Pieter is waiting by our plane and beckoning us to hurry. We get out of the car for the 500-metre walk through a paddock to the runway. Markus, our German delegate, says: 'Just walk slowly, look relaxed and don't look back!' I feel prickling twinges along my backbone as we walk. We are being watched suspiciously from the gate, their guns drawn, thinking nothing of planting a few bullets our way. No one would know, and no one would be accountable.

Pieter starts the engine and we take off: 'Just in time,' he says. 'We shall make it to Addis by sunset.'

Postscript

2007: Ethiopian military crackdown in the Ogaden with Al-Shabab militants attacking villages.
2011: US delegation cites the Ogaden as similar to hostilities in Dafur.

Baboon Encounter in the Fantale Crater, Ethiopia (1996)

'Expect the unexpected'

OSCAR WILDE

We find Goodluck, our genial Ethiopian driver, through the owners of a family-run hotel we use in Addis Ababa. Goodluck speaks some English and assures us that his rusted and dented four-wheel drive is sturdy and safe for our three-day safari to the Rift Valley and the crater in the Awash National Park.

It is 1996, and Ethiopia is slowly emerging from Mengistu's terror regime, with a fledgling tourism industry marketing the wonders of Ethiopia but restricted by basic or non-existent facilities. A luxury caravan site is perched on the rim of Fantale Crater. We are told this is the place to stay to view this geographic wonder of the Rift Valley, so we book a caravan. Goodluck has his sleeping bag and will stretch out overnight in his four-wheel drive. The Awash National Park is only three hours' drive from Addis and encompasses 400 square miles of acacia woods and grasslands. The Awash River, rapids and waterfalls wind through its base. The landscape rises to the crater's rim with a sheer drop into its core.

We slowly feel the rise in temperature as we descend from the heights of Addis at 2500 metres above sea level to 1000 metres at the Rift Valley. The temperature is now around 40°C. We cross the rail-line link between Addis and Djibouti,

and find the entrance to the national park, manned by neatly dressed rangers. After lengthy and ponderous ID reveals, and much stamping of documents, there is a parting of cash, which I suspect will go straight into their pockets.

We finally drive on through the park in search of the luxury caravan site. It is late afternoon, and there are skittish zebra interacting with each other, kicking, sparring and swishing their tails. We spot beautiful antelope nearby, a solitary nyala and a herd of Menelik's bushbuck. They are startled by our presence and stand motionless in the hope of camouflaging themselves against our intrusion into their territory. We bump and swerve around potholes on the dusty track, and finally arrive at the campsite. Five caravans, tyreless and sitting on rusted wheel rims, sit gently slanted towards the edge of a precipice that falls to the crater's floor. A small building with a balustraded terrace, a water tank and separate outhouse lie even closer to the crater's edge, to maximise the extraordinary view.

There is no one to welcome us, but Goodluck tells us that staff will arrive soon to cook, and a small group of German birdwatchers will be joining us for dinner. We carefully select the cleanest caravan; it has a double bed and mosquito nets but nothing else. We shall have to rely on parkas and picnic rugs to fend off nightfall's drop in temperature. We see a cloud of dust approaching the camp and a minibus emerges, spilling out the German birdwatchers, and at the same time a truck full of staff arrive and unpack crates of food to prepare dinner.

Clouds are billowing into black monsters over the horizon as the sun casts red light into the apertures of the crater and then drops like a stone. A golden sunset remains briefly before the clouds regroup in bulbous humps. Distant rumbles of thunder begin as we assemble for dinner, basic omelettes or *injera* with spicy meat sauce, black tea and more black tea. The German group is less than impressed, but Ethiopian beer is now flowing and soon the atmosphere is relaxed and happy. Their hair-raising travel tales of adventures in Ethiopia are becoming more embellished as the beer flows.

I misunderstand a question and I answer: 'We are staying here for a month.' The reaction of stark horror this brings, makes me realise they think we are staying in the caravan for a month. I clarify this, and then we hear about their train ride from Djibouti, and trying to sleep at a railway siding where the train stops overnight with an alcohol-fuelled party of locals singing and dancing until dawn.

We finally bid the group farewell as they set off for Addis in their minibus. The staff depart too, and so the three of us – Goodluck, the disciple and your author – are left alone with nature's elements about to deliver the most spectacular African storm I have ever seen. We sit on the terrace to watch the multi-forks of lightning streak the sky and thunderclaps respond. The whole crater seems to ignite with each flash and a full moon in clear sky to the north casts a ghostly and mystical light on the bushland around us.

Goodluck, chain-smoking strong cigarettes and agitated about the violent storm, bids us goodnight with a brisk retreat to his car. We decide it is time to brave the caravan as the first gigantic drops of rain fall. There is a lightning flash and a thunderclap vibrates the ground around us. We run to the van and remain in our shorts and T-shirts, the disciple trying to secure the mozzie nets as we roll up in parkas and picnic blankets, the caravan shuddering to the turmoil outside.

The slant of the caravan gives the disciple a sleepless night. He has nightmares of rolling down into the crater. I am so exhausted by the excitement of today's adventures, that sleep carries me through till dawn. The storm has passed and the cold of the night retreats with sunrise.

Goodluck suggests we head down to the Awash River to spend the heat of the day under shady trees; already the temperature is nearing 35°C. We have fruit and water, and Goodluck is well supplied with cigarettes, so after making coffee in the restaurant, we bundle everything into the car and head down the dusty track through heavily wooded terrain to the river valley below. We soon hear the rapids and take a track that borders the river.

Decades of turbulence in Ethiopia has deterred tourists and even now, with relative peace, there is only a trickle of people prepared to discover this remote and beautiful country. We feel wonderfully isolated and select a grassy clearing shaded by the huge fig trees that dominate this riverine area of the park.

Goodluck parks the car and is happy to relax in the shade with his cigarettes, while the disciple grabs bird books and maps to pore over. I take a rug and walk 15 metres away, spreading it out to the water's edge. I plan to sunbake a little and listen to birdsong and the rush of water over the rocks. Suddenly there is the sound of cracking twigs and a bush nearby shakes violently as a large baboon approaches me. I slowly sit up then remain still, and to my amazement he sits on the edge of the rug watching me. I guess he is a Savannah baboon, magnificent to look at, with his glossy coat, and eyes clear and keen.

Savannah baboons are prolific in Ethiopia and usually belong to a troop of between eight and 100 animals. They are diurnal and will take a siesta in hot weather, so no doubt I have disturbed his midday nap. He seems curious and yet relaxed and, after some time, he gets up and walks back to the large bush, returning with a female who has a small baby clinging to her neck with one arm. The baby gives me a quizzical look with sharp and mischievous eyes. The mother sits comfortably, just touching the male at her side, and the baby peeps at me over her shoulder as he climbs onto her back.

They sit on the edge of my rug. It is as if the father is showing off his female and baby for me to admire. I slowly and gently talk to them in a low voice and tell them how beautiful they are. There is absolutely no fear or tension between us and, as I don't have food with me, I can only conclude that curiosity has prompted them to join me. After ten minutes of sitting there regarding me, the male turns and heads back into the bush with his female and the baby close behind.

This experience has a profound effect on me. It confirms my theory, with no basis in science, that animals can sense love and gentleness in humans. I regale the men with my story, to a semi-interested reaction, but find that I am on a high for the rest of the day, immersed in my own thoughts and theories. We peel oranges and demolish packets of biscuits for lunch and then decide it's time to begin our long journey to the walled city of Harar, in eastern Ethiopia, where we plan to meet the tame hyenas that come to the town wall at sunset to be fed.

As we drive past my baboon meeting place, we see the flash of a large tail at least two metres long, attached to an even longer body. A huge and obviously well fed crocodile has also been enjoying the solitude of this place, sunning himself on a rock so close to us that it's probably best to move our thoughts to our next destination, rather than reflect too deeply on what might have been.

Fred Hollows and the Road to Axum, Ethiopia (1997)

'I studied medicine, so I could help others'

FRED HOLLOWS

We are approaching Asmara airport after an unscheduled stop in Riyadh, clutching the armrests as the Rift Valley's famous cross winds challenge our plane to land. This is finally achieved with a lurch, squeal of tyres and the roar of reverse thrust.

Marg, a dear friend and intrepid traveller, has joined me. We are hoping to see the Fred Hollows lens laboratory as well as the delights of Asmara, before making a road trip safari by crossing the Rift Valley and heading south into Ethiopia. Like Addis Ababa, Asmara was settled at high altitude and lies on the eastern rim of the Eritrean highlands, escaping the extreme heat and humidity of lower climes. After WWII, the British took power, replacing the Italians as colonists. They gave Ethiopia the reins in 1950, resulting in decades of unrest and vicious fighting. Eritrea finally became independent in 1991.

We disembark, and the atmosphere is calm and friendly with smiles of welcome from airport staff. Asmara's colonial architecture is a display of Italianate splendour, palm trees line the streets, there are groomed hedges and a town square named Piazza Roma Asmara. You would swear you were in Italy. We drive to the hotel admiring the blossoming shrubs, and elegant colonial buildings. It is hard to believe this is Eritrea, one of the poorest and most war-ravaged countries in Africa. 'Apparently they fight everywhere except Asmara,' says Marg.

Our once grand hotel is shabby. We notice the crowds of women from all over Africa milling in the foyer, the glorious coloured turbans, cloaks and kaftans, Moslem scarves and burkas, worn with elegance and style. Standing to one side surveying this excitement is an elderly woman, simply dressed in linens, with a beautiful silk scarf knotted at her neck. She approaches us and we discover that she has organised this African Women's Conference. We later hear that her name is Rothschild, and she has, in fact, financed the conference and paid fares and accommodation for all delegates to attend. In some cases dangerous subterfuge has been used, by disguising delegates as men for safe passage through countries where women are forbidden to travel. The work she does in Africa is quiet, significant and entirely anonymous.

We readily accept an invitation to attend the conference as observers. The idea of the conference is to unite African women, and to allow those who are living with political anarchy and gender suppression to gain strength through other women, exchanging their stories and ideas, forming bonds and networks that will hopefully channel them towards practical solutions back home.

Eritrea has been chosen as the venue because it is a newly independent country, with credit given to the expertise of the female soldiers in gaining victory. Now the war is over, Eritrean women are demanding equal status and rights. 'We fought with men for independence, now we can work together' is their mantra.

Each country's delegate speaks on women's issues in their

country. Topics cover female circumcision, child brides, education, and primary health care. The Eritrean delegate is in a wheelchair. During the war she stepped on a landmine and her legs were blown off. This inspiring speaker is young and dynamic with a beautiful expressive face. Languages and dialects are sorted by interpreters. The conference exposes the challenges women face in Africa today. It is fascinating to see these diverse cultures and religions all noisily working together in the room, with a common goal of instigating change for all women to lead healthy and happy lives. We are well aware of the privilege in attending such a remarkable event.

We spend the next morning gowned, masked and scrubbed visiting the Fred Hollows Intraocular Lens Laboratory, which opened in 1994. Australian eye surgeon Fred Hollows realised the devastating challenge of cataract blindness in Eritrea while working on eyes at the war's frontline in the late 1980s. When hostilities ended he decided to establish an intraocular lens laboratory in newly independent Eritrea that could supply high quality lenses for cataract surgery all over Africa.

The laboratory was built in Asmara to First World standards, with training courses in cataract surgery made available to African doctors. Fred Hollows died in 1993, and is a legend of god-like importance in this country. Every family knows of someone who can now see, having been cured of cataract blindness. The name Hollows has become a common Christian name for boys in Eritrea; no doubt this personal acknowledgement would have touched Fred deeply. The laboratory has been in operation for three years, exporting lenses all over Africa and establishing Eritrea as the centre of excellence for eye health and cataract procedures.

Abey's name means 'father's joy' in Amharic, and we can see he lives up to his moniker with a personality that radiates fun and laughter. His attempts to speak English are accompanied by wild gestures, facial gymnastics and a helpless shrug of shoulders to seek our sympathy. He is happy to drive us to Axum, where he is a tour guide and driver. Having brought delegates to Asmara for the conference, he is pleased to have paying passengers for his return home.

Axum is 180 kilometres from Asmara in the Tigray Region of Ethiopia. This is a short drive, but we plan to spend most of the day en route to take in the magnitude of the Rift Valley. Even the Grand Canyon is dwarfed by this geographic masterpiece, a 6000-kilometre trench extending from Syria to Mozambique. On leaving Asmara we shall drive through the Afar Depression, 100-kilometres wide and a World Heritage-listed wonder.

We leave early in the morning and drive along well-graded gravel roads, a legacy of Mussolini, who built and road-mapped Ethiopia strategically when the Italians were in control during WWII. Today Ethiopians will proudly tell you about the Battle of Adwa in 1896, where the Italians were heroically defeated by the Ethiopians. They will boast that it's Africa's only victory against European colonists and marked their liberation from Fascist occupation.

Before long we see the Rift Valley stretching across the horizon. Shadows delineate sheer cliff faces that drop to the valley floor. We are still at high altitude, around 2100 metres above sea level, and Abey stops the car so we can walk to rocky boulders at the roadside. We sit in silence. The air is clear, the sky blue and unsullied by pollution. The only sign of human interference is the gravel road ahead. 'It's as if we are the only life on earth!' says Marg. But suddenly, flapping wings and caws from a flock of vultures pass above us. They are scanning the landscape in search of carrion. We descend the escarpment to the valley floor passing goatherds tended by children, and in the distance we see a cluster of conical and thatched *tukul* dwellings, signifying their village home.

It is a slow drive to Adi Kwala, a small town near the border with Ethiopia. We stop and accept an invitation for traditional Ethiopian coffee made by two beautiful girls wearing cream hemp dresses with brightly embroidered borders, their tightly braided hair accentuating glorious high cheek bones. The coffee is infused in a decorative pot that sits on an iron tripod over a small pile of glowing embers. We sit around the fire on low stools as the coffee brews, with Abey showing off his expertise as interpreter. The coffee is served in small fly mugs with a pinch of cardamom and sugar, the brew thick, aromatic and delicious. The roadside cafe is busy with local trade, as well as a few tourists.

We drive to the border and notice a daunting line of checkpoint booths, and a roadblock with a chain attached to steel poles. A uniformed guard directs us to stop. We look across the roadblock and see 100 metres of no-man's-land, and then another line of booths flying the Ethiopian flag. This is not a bustling border and we sense that we are giving bored officials something to occupy their day and a lengthy process awaits us.

Two hours later we drive across the border into Ethiopia. We stifled impatience and irritation with the process of each booth manager analysing papers, visas and passports, requiring more form filling, then producing stamps of all sizes and colours

to imprint authority on each statement, before directing us to the next booth for similar scrutiny. Abey was briskly assessed and stamped and waited patiently for us by the car, smoking his cigarettes.

There is a dusky-pink twilight as we finally arrive in Axum, and find our hotel has no power or running water. The rooms are candlelit, and there is a condom on each pillow, one way that Ethiopia is actively trying to repel the frightening AIDS epidemic currently sweeping through Africa. A bucket of water sits in the corner of our room for washing hands. Mosquito nets hang from the ceilings over narrow iron beds, with even narrower mattresses. There are no sheets, but a neatly folded blanket and one pillow each.

We have a little porch with a dimly lit lantern hooked above the door, and after a hand wash and face scrub, we take a winding path through dense gardens and overhanging creepers to the dining room. The choice is goat meat barbecued to a cinder, or omelettes. We find Ethiopian beer a welcome refuge, and call it dessert.

It's obvious that Axum has yet to recover from wars and famine, and life here is spartan. Sleep is difficult with noisy mozzies attacking the nets until dawn, but delightful and friendly staff try to ensure we are comfortable, with no facilities at all, and make our stay unforgettable.

Axum is an extraordinary place of mystery and legend. It is said to be the home of the Queen of Sheba and to house the Ark of the Covenant, and is the holy centre of the Orthodox Church in Ethiopia, boasting two cathedrals. The city is dotted with carved granite obelisks from the 4th century marking graves and tombs. Abey takes us to the chapel where the Ark

of the Covenant is said to lie, and we discover that no one is allowed entry, whether they be crowned heads or paupers, but we can marvel at the bright frescoes that adorn the foyer. This icon is in the sole charge of a guardian monk. The Queen of Sheba's bath is more like a small dam, and steep steps down to green and turgid water mark her grand entrance. We imagine King Solomon loitering close by. These myths, legends and superstitions intertwine to form an intrinsic part of cultural life, central to the Orthodox religion in Ethiopia today.

We farewell Abey at the Axum airstrip, where an ancient-looking plane, belching oil from a propeller, is about to take us to Addis. The road to Axum has far exceeded our expectations.

Postscript

Between 1998 and 2000 there was a senseless war in this region and 100,000 Eritreans and Ethiopians lost their lives. There now exists a precarious truce, but the road has been seeded with landmines, and is too dangerous for wandering tourists.

Lake Tana, Ethiopia (2000)

*'All streams carry the wisdom of forests to the lake,
where silence replaces noise'*

MEHMET ILDAN

The disciple and I are taking a round trip of northern Ethiopia, having spent time with Catherine at the Fistula Hospital in Addis Ababa. We have seen the rock-hewn churches of Lalibela and spent a few days hiking, riding donkeys and using our own two feet, but always with an Ethiopian guide to help us on our way.

The disciple has become a folk hero with the kids of Lalibela, playing table tennis with them, and organising teams and tournaments. The table is set up on a rocky terrace near the market square, and each morning we have a fleet of children following us pestering for more games. Ten-year-old Amir makes a point of speaking English with me. I notice his words and Victorian-era phrases, and ask him where he learnt to speak English. 'A Bible was beget to me, and I read the Old Testament, so one day I shall lead tourists in Lalibela,' he says.

Tourism is beginning to grow, broadening the spectrum of visitors to Ethiopia. Backpackers add to the regular influx of European birdwatching groups, historians and religious zealots. Lalibela, Axum and Gondar are pillars of the Christian Orthodox church in Ethiopia, harbouring centuries of exquisite art, rock-hewn churches and monasteries.

Our northern circuit ends on the shores of Lake Tana at

the small town of Bahir Dar. Lake Tana marks the source of the River Nile, before its long journey through Sudan and Egypt to the Mediterranean Sea, and is a renowned destination for migratory birds. It is favoured by waders, storks and flamingoes, who feast on algae in the reed beds and wetlands along the lake's shoreline. There are also extensive papyrus beds from which local fishing boats or *tankwa* are built. This lakeside environment includes rocky crags and riverine forests, creating a mecca for migrating birds as well as a haven for local birdlife.

Bahir Dar has spectacular flame trees lining the streets. The orange-red fronds splay like sunsets on each tree, contrasting with the charcoal-grey clouds we bounced through, as we descended to the airstrip.

'Does this remind you of Thika?' I ask the disciple, who was born in Kenya.

'The Italians copied us!' he replies, referring to his Brit-colonial background, and claiming British town-planning superiority in Africa.

We decide to spend two days in Bahir Dar, and choose a rather dilapidated hotel on the lake's shoreline, a perfect location for a day of birdwatching. We are not alone in our birdlife fascination. It's a weekend tradition for local families to gather here with picnic baskets and rugs, taking up position under the trees and on the grassy slopes that lead to the lake. We choose the trunk of an enormous fig tree (Ficus vasta) as a backrest, and spread out towels and cushions, lying back in comfort to watch the pantomime above us.

There are at least 40 vultures in our fig tree, and their aggressive wing flapping and deafening cawing ensures that no other birds dare approach, which today seems to be a vulture stronghold. They are very large birds, boasting long necks with sharp eyes glinting from bald heads, and a luxuriant plumage of black and white feathers; their wings span two metres. Vultures are the proud and necessary scavengers of Africa but, today, this fig tree seems a meeting place of minds. There are spats over favoured branches, and sparring battles over prospective partners are sorting out the pecking order within the group.

Waders and storks strut at the water's edge selecting delicacies among the reeds. On the banks shrubs and bushes rustle with birdlife, and loud whistles and cheeps punctuate the day's agenda. Suddenly the squeal and roar of fighter jets assault our senses, as they swoop over the lake and circle, a swathe of dirty exhaust fumes streaming from their engines. They are MIGs, discarded by Russia and subsequently sold to Ethiopia. We later discover that Russian pilots are training Ethiopians to fly them. It is a horrible and noisy reminder of human conflict. When the jets finally disappear over the horizon, the lake's birdsong slowly and tentatively returns.

Teferi is a driver, tour guide and odd job man at the hotel, and he invites us to take a sunset cruise in his reed *tankwa* with an egg-beater engine latched to the back and a couple of oars thrown in for good measure. He will navigate. We gingerly step in, hoping this fragile-looking dinghy can withstand ambush by hippos or crocodiles.

The sun is low in the sky and a gentle breeze whips up ripples on the glassy water as we head for one of twenty islands on Lake Tana, chosen as religious sites in the 14th century. These islands house monasteries and churches, the most famous being Kibran Island, said to have held the Ark of the Covenant, before it was transferred to Axum. We land on the island and

squelch through muddy reed beds onto a path that leads to an ancient church perched on a small hill. We are met by an agitated monk, who emphatically gestures that we must leave the island at once.

'Probably it's because no women are allowed in the church, and he thinks this rule should apply to the island as well,' says Teferi.

We return to the boat as the sun is setting. We need to head back to the hotel before dark. We putt-putt through water shimmering with pink, reflecting the dying sun. Suddenly we hear the hippos harrumphing to each other, their huge heads emerging from the depths with much swishing and splashing, before they disappear below the surface, leaving their prominent eye bumps just above the waterline. 'They are watching us', says Teferi. Fortunately they are ten metres from our boat, and we avoid an ambush. Hippos are very territorial and can be dangerous. They are annually credited with more human deaths than any other animal in the wild.

Six elephants saunter along the shoreline as wading birds select their final delicacies amongst the reeds before nightfall. Teferi moors the *tankwa* and suggests we attend tonight's traditional Ethiopian feast set up in the gardens of the hotel overlooking Lake Tana. The gardens are lit by lanterns dangling from trees that line the pathway to the banquet setting; tables are spread with *injera*, rolled into neat lines beside ornate copper tureens. There are lit candles and garlands of flowers draping the tables. The spicy smell of food mixed with heady perfumes of frangipani and jasmine is an intoxicating mix.

Injera, the highly nutritious national dish, is a sour-dough flatbread made from teff, the grain that flourishes in the

Ethiopian highlands. It tastes tart and is spongy in texture, with a rather uninviting pale-grey colouring, but rolled and dipped into spicy meat or vegetable sauces it is delicious. Sweet fruit juices of pomegranate and mango are served, as well as local beer. The disciple swears it is the best tasting beer in Africa. Platters of sugary cakes and sweets are later served with strong coffee that has been roasted and brewed in true Ethiopian style over a small coal fire nearby.

We listen to musicians playing lute-like instruments accompanied by a beautiful girl with tightly braided hair, singing Amharic love songs. She wears a traditional dress of cream hemp, embroidered in bold colours, and belted with a flamboyant sash. This sets the mood of nostalgia for the locals and an exotic other-worldness for foreigners.

There is a table of Russian pilots nearby. They have been training Ethiopians to fly the MIGs, and are taking a weekend break from their airbase digs. They are chasing vodka shots with beer, punctuated by loud toasts and long and emotional speeches. We decide that it is time to fade from the scene, and so I turn to their table as we pass to say: *'Do svidaniya!'* – 'goodbye' in Russian, a distant memory from early ballet classes in Adelaide. My teacher closed each class with *do svidaniya* accompanied by a deep bow. Their response is a chorus of cheery *do svidaniya!*

We slowly weave our way up the lantern-lit pathway to our room on the terrace, to fight with a dysfunctional shower, set up mozzie nets – hopefully minus holes – and spray Rid around flyscreens in an effort to ensure a relatively peaceful night. Around midnight there is a persistent rap at our door. The disciple is asleep so I open the latch to see one of the Russian pilots with tears flowing down his cheeks, holding photos of his wife and children. Thinking I speak Russian, he wants to come in and show off his family photos.

The disciple awakes and we invite the pilot in, saying, 'No speak Russian!'

But we gesture him to sit down at the table, and he does so, lovingly setting out his photos. We see his beautiful Russian wife with a chubby six-month-old baby and a curly-haired toddler, pictured at home in Moscow, at his parents' *dacha,*, and on holiday in Crimea. He is a little worse for wear, but obviously lonely and sick of being so far from home. Despite having no common language, we are able to admire his family and make him laugh.

The disciple jumps around the table imitating a kangaroo, trying to explain our home is Australia, and then shows him photos of our two boys on a surf beach. There is a surreal empathy between us as we share photos of loved ones who are living literally poles apart. Our midnight visitor is smiling now, more relaxed in our company. Through sign language and gestures we gather he has another six weeks to train pilots before returning home to Russia. He finally gets up from the table, gently gathers his precious photos and bows to the disciple and kisses my hand as he bids us *do svidaniya*.

This brief encounter has been special, and we sit in silence on the terrace, watching the moonlight play with ripples on the lake, immersed in our own thoughts and reluctant to leave Lake Tana.

Tracking Predators in South Africa

'There is no forgiveness in nature'

UGO BETTI

It is 2005 and I am joining a five-week wildlife expedition as a research volunteer at Edeni Game Reserve in South Africa. The reserve covers 9000 hectares and was established as a conservancy in 1998. The focus will be on predator–prey relationships and density, kill frequencies and range use by predators. These studies are invaluable for the successful running of game reserves in Africa and data from this project is monitored closely to help maintain the correct balance of predator to prey, and to conserve unique habitats.

The little turboprop plane descends over the Blyde River Canyon of the Drakensberg Mountains to land at Hoedspruit airport near Kruger National Park. I see a giraffe sauntering through the bush near the runway as we taxi to the small terminal. Richard, the research team's naturalist, throws my bag into the back of his ute. His stories of reptiles, bugs and butterflies enliven the ride over dusty roads to Edeni.

The camp is an old Afrikaner farmhouse with dormitories and basic amenities, plus a sublime garden with an African *kappa*-style gazebo and small pool. We volunteers will run the camp, cooking included. We start intensive training to learn to calculate GPS readings, work the telemetry equipment and

record data. It is intensely hot. Ceiling fans provide the only respite and whirr noisily all night. We have been told to close our door because hyenas skulk around the camp at night, but at 40°C the choice between sleeping in a sauna and risking a hyena encounter is easy. The door stays open.

The rosters are in place and vehicle duty is at 4.30 am. I must check oil, water and tyres by torchlight and hope that the hyenas and spiders and snakes are fast asleep. Then, it's off to fill the backpack with water, suntan lotion, energy bars, binoculars and two cameras, get the GPS and telemetry equipment, drink a quick coffee in the kitchen and go out to join Ranger Tish in the open truck. Our mission today is tracking cheetah and leopard. The predators have microchips and we shall track their frequency with the telemetry aerial. I sit with Kelli in the back, holding the aerial high. Tish drives with Matt in front recording the data. The sky is promising sunrise as we race along bumpy tracks, in and out of creek beds, as eagles and vultures circle above us. Impala scatter and giraffe stare as we follow the beeps, now registering minus five, the highest rating for proximity. We stop the truck and walk in line with Tish, who is armed and leading the way.

There they are, two male cheetah, lying close together, seemingly relaxed and content. We need to ascertain if there has been a kill, identify the carcass and make a stomach-fill rating from one to five. Both males ignore us, their bellies protruding, probably a three rating. There is no carcass nearby. We reluctantly return to the truck to track the next predator.

We come across an elephant herd, with two subadults misbehaving and kicking up dust at each other. The matriarch of the herd charges them, trumpeting with her trunk held high,

and the youngsters stop immediately. Five hours of tracking ends back at camp with breakfast and a swim, before a three-hour game walk.

At 4 pm the evening research drive begins. A pattern emerges where I become used to little sleep and the heat and dust. I am now totally mesmerised by the animals. Will the leopard make a kill tonight to be able to feed her hungry cub? Will the young male lions survive, now that they are away from the pride?

Constante, our ranger, has been radioed about a young lion in distress. A snake has been seen near him. We drive to the riverbed, and the lion is darted and lifted onto a mattress in the ute. We meet the vet who sets up a saline drip and finds no snake bite, but a bone shard lodged in the lion's gum. It has caused severe infection. The young lion is given antibiotics and we take him to a protected area to recover. One week later he is back with his pride: without this help he would have died.

We deal with poaching, rogue elephants and an orphaned cheetah, and every day brings a new dimension to life in the wild. For five weeks I see neither newspapers nor television, our complete focus is on the animals in our care.

This has been a life-changing experience.

Epilogue

Writing these adventures from many remote corners of our magical planet, has reinforced my belief that we must retain our childish curiosity, and blindly take risks to find out more. Complacency is kryptonite. The more curious we are, the more adventurous we become, and it is then that extraordinary revelations and insights into humanity and wildlife are possible.

In the most dire of circumstances, human resilience, children's laughter, stoicism, and humour always seem to shine through.

It seems the grim message of climate change and our world's overpopulation is being slowly understood and countered by positive forces. Even with the horrors of rhino poaching and other wildlife extinctions, there are forces gathering with the aid of internet education, that reveal a flickering light at the end of the tunnel. I believe a balance between human life and wildlife is possible, and that a positive future awaits our children's children.

Wakefield Press is an independent publishing and
distribution company based in Adelaide, South Australia.
We love good stories and publish beautiful books.
To see our full range of books, please visit our website at
www.wakefieldpress.com.au
where all titles are available for purchase.

Find us!

Twitter: www.twitter.com/wakefieldpress
Facebook: www.facebook.com/wakefield.press
Instagram: instagram.com/wakefieldpress